Affiliate Marketing for Beginners 2025

A Step-By-Step Guide to Affiliate Marketing, Making Passive Income, and Growing Your Online Business

MARK LANDON

Available formats: Kindle eBook | Paperback | Hardcover | Audiobook (free with 30-day trial on Audible.com)

Book Contents

INTRODUCTION

Affiliate marketing has long been a staple in the digital landscape as a strategy to promote products and generate revenue through commission-based partnerships, involving affiliates and merchants.

Affiliate marketing supports a passive income business model. Bloggers, YouTubers, social media marketers, and other types of affiliates create content that exists indefinitely and is available online 24/7. Therefore, sales and commissions can occur throughout the day, regardless of the affiliate's work schedule.

Drawing upon real-world examples and expert insights, this book equips affiliate marketers, entrepreneurs, and digital enthusiasts with the knowledge and tools necessary to scale their businesses and harness the transformative power of ChatGPT in their affiliate marketing endeavors. For instance, affiliates can use ChatGPT to increase their productivity, allowing them to produce more content quicker and distribute more links.

Chapters one to three cover essential affiliate marketing concepts, necessary skills, keys to success, and getting started.

Chapters four and five focus on affiliate business models, link promotion, marketing tools, content, and traffic sources.

Chapters six to eight reviews affiliate marketing software, networks, programs, considerations, and recommendations. We also explore cost-per-action models, commission structures, payments, and secondary income streams.

Chapters nine and ten focus on the convergence of ChatGPT and affiliate marketing, exploring the synergies that emerge when these two powerful forces combine. We review their inner workings and immense potential as a tool for developing authentic content and driving affiliate sales.

Chapters eleven and twelve conclude the book and address frequently asked questions from new and experienced affiliate marketers.

Whether you're an affiliate marketer looking to unlock a competitive edge, a business owner seeking to amplify your online presence, or an AI enthusiast intrigued by the possibilities of ChatGPT, this book serves as your guide to navigating the intersection of affiliate marketing and artificial intelligence.

Together, let us embark on this transformative journey, where the limitless potential of ChatGPT reshapes the landscape of digital commerce and revolutionizes how we engage with customers in the affiliate marketing arena.

<Chapter 1>

AFFILIATE MARKETING FOR BEGINNERS

Affiliate marketing is one of the most straightforward online money-making methods, appealing to thousands of digital entrepreneurs. It primarily involves creating content and adding unique links to your content. This chapter explores affiliate and digital marketing fundamentals to get you going in the right direction. Also, we cover how much affiliates can make.

What Is Affiliate Marketing?

Affiliate marketing is a performance-based marketing strategy in which individuals or companies, known as affiliates or publishers, promote products or services on behalf of a merchant or advertiser. Affiliates earn a commission for each sale, lead, or action generated through their promotional efforts.

The beauty of affiliate marketing lies in its win-win nature. Merchants benefit from expanded reach and increased sales without incurring upfront marketing costs. At the same time, affiliates can monetize their online presence or marketing skills by promoting products or services that align with their audience's interests. Consumers also benefit from affiliate marketing as they gain access to relevant products or services recommended by trusted sources.

Affiliate marketing has evolved into a multi-billion dollar industry with many niches and business models. It is a flexible and scalable approach to online marketing, allowing individuals and businesses of all sizes to participate and generate passive income. Whether through niche blogs, social media influencers, coupon websites, or review platforms, affiliate marketing has become an integral part of the digital landscape, offering a mutually beneficial arrangement for all parties involved.

How Affiliate Marketing Works

The affiliate marketing ecosystem typically involves three key players: the merchant or advertiser, the affiliate, and the consumer. The merchant or advertiser is the entity that offers a product or service for sale. The affiliate acts as a middleman, promoting the merchant's products or services through various marketing channels, such as websites, blogs, social media, or email marketing. The consumer is the end user who purchases or takes the desired action.

Affiliates earn commissions by driving traffic and conversions to the merchant's website. They utilize the merchant's unique tracking links or codes to identify and attribute sales or actions to their specific marketing efforts. When a consumer clicks on an affiliate's tracking link and makes a purchase or completes a desired action, such as signing up for a newsletter or filling out a form, the affiliate is credited with the referral and earns a commission based on a predetermined percentage or flat rate.

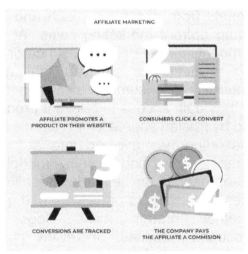

Image: Freepik.com

Overview of Digital Marketing

Affiliate marketing is one of many digital marketing strategies businesses use to increase sales. Digital marketing uses digital channels and technologies to promote products, services, or brands. It encompasses a wide range of tactics and strategies to reach and engage target audiences online. In today's increasingly connected world, digital marketing has become vital to any successful marketing campaign.

Businesses employ various strategies in their digital marketing efforts, depending on their goals, target audience, and available resources. Also, affiliate marketers use digital marketing strategies and tools to grow their revenues. Some of the most common digital marketing strategies include:

Search engine optimization (SEO) focuses on optimizing a website's visibility in search engine results pages. By improving website structure, content quality, and relevancy, businesses aim to rank higher in search engine listings and increase organic (non-paid) traffic.

Pay-per-click advertising (PPC) involves placing paid ads on search engines, social media platforms, or other websites. Advertisers pay a fee each time a user clicks on their ads. Popular PPC platforms include Google Ads, Bing Ads, and social media advertising platforms like YouTube, Facebook, Instagram, and LinkedIn.

Content marketing involves creating and distributing valuable, relevant, and engaging content to attract and retain a target audience. This can include blog posts, articles, videos, infographics, podcasts, webinars, and more. The goal is to build brand awareness, establish authority, and nurture customer relationships.

Social media marketing utilizes social media platforms such as Facebook, Twitter, Instagram, LinkedIn, and YouTube to promote products or services. Businesses engage with their audience, share content, run ads, and foster meaningful connections to drive brand awareness, engagement, and conversions.

Email marketing involves sending targeted messages to a subscriber list to nurture leads, build customer loyalty, and drive conversions. It can include newsletters, promotional campaigns, personalized recommendations, and automated email sequences to engage with customers at different sales funnel stages.

Influencer marketing leverages the popularity and reach of influencers, individuals with a significant online following, to promote products or services. Businesses collaborate with influencers to tap into their audience and benefit from their credibility and influence.

Conversion rate optimization (CRO) focuses on improving the effectiveness of a website or landing page in converting visitors into customers. Businesses optimize their online assets through A/B testing, user experience enhancements, and data analysis to maximize conversions and revenue.

As discussed earlier, affiliate marketing is a strategy where businesses collaborate with affiliates to promote their products or services. Affiliates earn a commission for each sale or action they generate through marketing efforts.

These are just a few examples of the many digital marketing strategies available. Businesses often combine multiple tactics, tailor their approach to their target audience, and continuously adapt their strategy based on market trends, customer behavior, and performance analytics. The dynamic nature of digital marketing allows businesses to connect with their audiences more personalized, measurable, and cost-effectively than traditional marketing methods.

How Much Can You Make?

The earning potential of an affiliate marketer can vary significantly and depends on various factors such as the niche, the affiliate program, the marketing strategies employed, the level of effort invested, and market conditions. It is important to note that affiliate marketing is not a get-rich-quick scheme, and success requires dedication, patience, and continuous effort.

Some affiliate marketers may earn only a modest income, while others can achieve substantial earnings. In some cases, top-performing affiliates can generate six or even seven-figure revenues annually. However, it is vital to approach income expectations with realistic perspectives.

The commission structure of affiliate programs can vary, typically ranging from a few percent to 50% or more of the sale value. Additionally, the volume and quality of traffic you can drive and the conversion rates play a significant role in determining earnings. Building a loyal and engaged audience, leveraging effective marketing strategies, and optimizing click-through rates are vital factors that can contribute to higher profits.

It's also worth noting that affiliate marketing offers the potential for passive income. Once you have established a successful affiliate marketing system, it is possible to generate income even when you're not actively working. This passive income potential can contribute to long-term financial stability and scalability.

Ultimately, the earnings of an affiliate marketer are highly individual and can vary greatly. It's essential to set realistic expectations, continuously improve your marketing skills, adapt to market trends, and persistently work towards maximizing your income potential.

Transparency & Disclosures

When engaging in affiliate marketing, it's essential to maintain transparency and comply with disclosure guidelines. These guidelines vary by country, but here are some general principles to consider:

FTC Guidelines (United States): The Federal Trade Commission (FTC) requires affiliates to disclose their relationships with advertisers in the United States. When promoting products or services through affiliate links, you must declare any business relationships or conflicts of interest. Disclosures should be clear, prominent, and easily understood by your audience.

Clear and Conspicuous Disclosures: Disclosures should be placed where they are easily noticeable and understandable by your audience. They should be close to the affiliate link or recommendation and not buried within long paragraphs or small font sizes.

Use Clear Language: Disclosures should be written in plain and understandable language. Avoid using ambiguous or vague terms that may confuse your audience. Clearly state that you may earn a commission or compensation when users purchase through your affiliate links.

Disclose Before Affiliate Links: Disclose your affiliate relationship before users click on your affiliate links. This allows them to make an informed decision before engaging with the promoted product or service.

Disclose on All Relevant Platforms: Ensure that disclosures are present on all platforms where you promote affiliate products or services. This includes websites, blogs, social media channels, emails, videos, and other affiliate marketing mediums.

Prominence and Visibility: Disclosures should be easily noticeable and stand out visually. Use a font size and color that is visible against the background. Avoid placing disclosures in a location where they may be easily overlooked.

Long-Lasting Disclosures: If your content is evergreen or remains accessible over time, ensure that disclosures stay visible and relevant. For example, if you have a blog post with affiliate links, the disclosure should still be present even if the post is accessed months or years later.

Update Disclosures as Needed: If there are any changes to your affiliate relationships or compensation structure, update your disclosures accordingly to reflect the current state of your partnerships.

These guidelines are incomplete, and regulations may differ based on your location. It's crucial to familiarize yourself with the specific policies and regulations applicable to your country or region. Additionally, consider consulting legal professionals or industry experts for guidance on compliance with affiliate marketing disclosure requirements.

<Chapter 2>

IS AFFILIATE MARKETING RIGHT FOR YOU

Many people find affiliate marketing satisfying, but like entrepreneurship; it's not for everyone. That's why evaluating the benefits and drawbacks is critical, which we highlight in this chapter. Next, we pinpoint the necessary skills and the keys to affiliate marketing success to help you thrive and generate significant earnings. Finally, we explore a day in the life of an affiliate marketer and discuss the importance of transparency and disclosures to build trust with your audience.

Pros & Cons of Being an Affiliate Marketer

Being an affiliate marketer offers a range of benefits, but like any profession, it also has its challenges. Let's explore the pros and cons of being an affiliate marketer.

The benefits of being an affiliate marketer include the following:

Affiliate Marketing Is Simple: Affiliate marketers add links to their content and websites. Then, they generate sales commissions. Merchants also have practical rules for affiliates to follow. For example, publishers cannot use domains containing the merchant's name. That's a straightforward business and revenue model.

Low Startup Costs: Affiliate marketing generally has low barriers to entry. You don't need to create products, invest in inventory, or handle customer support. The initial investment primarily involves setting up a website or marketing platform and driving traffic through content creation, SEO, or paid advertising.

Passive Income Potential: Once you have established a successful affiliate marketing system, it can generate passive income. You can earn commissions without actively working with practical strategies and ongoing optimization.

Diverse Revenue Streams: You can promote products or services from multiple merchants across different niches as an affiliate marketer. This diversification allows you to tap into various revenue streams, reducing reliance on a single source of income.

Help People: Your content can inform and educate people, leading to wiser purchases. Also, content can entertain and delight audiences, making people much happier and more fulfilled.

Merchants Do the Hard Work: Will you make sales calls, provide customer service, or handle returns? No. Affiliate marketers don't do any of those things. Instead, your only responsibility is to promote companies, products, and services.

Develop In-Demand Skills: Affiliate marketing requires individuals to develop digital marketing skills, including content, email, and social media marketing, SEO, conversion rate optimization, advertising, website design, etc. Those capabilities are desirable in an expanding digital landscape.

Work Alone or Build a Team: Affiliate marketing allows you to work independently or hire others. For example, you might hire freelancers to assist you with graphic design, content creation, or website management. Upwork and Fiverr are two popular marketplaces for freelance services.

Access to Analytics and Data: Affiliate marketing provides access to detailed analytics and performance data. This enables you to measure the effectiveness of your campaigns, track conversions, and make data-driven decisions to optimize your marketing efforts.

Flexible Work Schedule: Affiliate marketing allows you to work on your terms. You can set your schedule, choose the products or services you want to promote and work from anywhere with an internet connection. This flexibility allows for a better work-life balance and the ability to pursue other interests.

The drawbacks of being an affiliate marketer include the following:

Variable Income and Uncertain Cash Flow: Affiliate marketing income can fluctuate significantly. It may take time to build a steady stream of commissions, and certain factors, such as changes in market trends or commission structures, can impact your earnings. It requires patience, perseverance, and the ability to manage your finances effectively.

Dependency on Affiliate Programs: As an affiliate marketer, your success is tied to the affiliate programs you join and support. If a program ends or changes its terms, commission, or cookie duration, it can affect your income. A merchant that doesn't pay will negatively impact you (that rarely happens on affiliate networks, though). Diversifying your affiliate partnerships can mitigate this risk.

Dependency on Affiliate Software: No affiliate marketing app can guarantee that all clicks and conversions are captured 100% of the time. Therefore, affiliates are subject to technical mishaps like everyone else who relies on business software and the Internet.

Competitive Landscape: The affiliate marketing industry is highly competitive. Finding profitable niches and competing with other affiliates requires in-depth research, strategic planning, and continuous adaptation to market trends.

Reliance on Traffic Generation: To generate affiliate sales, you must drive targeted traffic to your website or marketing platform. This requires expertise in SEO, content marketing, social media, paid advertising, or other traffic generation methods. Building and maintaining a consistent flow of traffic can be challenging and time-consuming.

Compliance and Legal Considerations: As an affiliate marketer, you must comply with various legal and ethical guidelines, such as disclosing affiliate relationships, adhering to advertising regulations, and respecting consumer privacy. Staying updated with these requirements and ensuring compliance can be a complex task.

It's essential to weigh these pros and cons when considering a career in affiliate marketing. While it offers numerous benefits and potential for success, it also requires dedication, adaptability, and the ability to navigate the ever-evolving digital landscape.

Essential Skills for Affiliate Marketers

To excel as an affiliate marketer, several essential skills can contribute to your success. Here are some critical skills and abilities to develop, depending on your marketing interests:

Digital Marketing Knowledge: A strong foundation in digital marketing is crucial for affiliate marketers. Understanding SEO, content marketing, social media marketing, paid advertising, email marketing, and conversion rate optimization is essential to drive targeted traffic, engage with audiences, and optimize conversions.

Content Creation and Copywriting: Creating compelling and high-quality content is integral to attracting and retaining an audience. Develop skills in writing engaging blog posts, articles, product reviews, email campaigns, social media posts, and other forms of content that effectively promote products or services.

Research and Analytical Skills: Affiliate marketers must conduct thorough market research, competitor analysis, and keyword research to identify profitable niches, target audiences and optimize their campaigns. Strong analytical skills are crucial for tracking and interpreting data, identifying trends, and making data-driven decisions to improve performance.

SEO and Keyword Optimization: Knowledge of search engine optimization techniques, including on-page and off-page optimization, keyword research, and link building, can help improve organic search rankings and drive targeted traffic to your affiliate content.

Relationship Building and Networking: Building relationships with affiliate managers, merchants, and other industry professionals can open doors to collaboration opportunities, exclusive offers, and valuable insights. Networking skills and establishing and nurturing professional connections can enhance your affiliate marketing career.

Conversion Rate Optimization (CRO): Understanding CRO principles, such as A/B testing, user experience optimization, website and landing page design, and persuasive copywriting, can help maximize conversions and revenue from your affiliate campaigns.

Digital Tools and Platforms: Familiarity with various digital marketing tools and platforms can streamline your affiliate marketing efforts. This includes content management systems (CMS), email marketing software, social media management tools, analytics platforms, and affiliate networks.

Communication and Persuasion Skills: Effective communication skills are essential for connecting with your audience, engaging with merchants, negotiating partnerships, and promoting products persuasively. Clear and persuasive messaging can significantly impact your conversion rates and success as an affiliate marketer.

Adaptability and Continuous Learning: The digital landscape is ever-changing, and staying updated with the latest industry trends, algorithm updates, and marketing strategies is crucial. Being adaptable, open to learning, and willing to embrace new technologies and techniques will help you stay ahead in the competitive affiliate marketing landscape.

Remember that acquiring these skills may require time, practice, and ongoing learning. Invest in self-education, online courses, industry conferences, and networking opportunities to continuously refine and expand your skillset as an affiliate marketer.

Keys to Affiliate Marketing Success

Affiliate marketing isn't complicated; if you follow these steps to success, you'll achieve your goals.

Partnerships: Partner with reputable merchants offering win-win affiliate programs, including attractive commission rates, fair referral periods, and reasonable payment thresholds. For example, Merchant ABC provides a 20% commission rate and a 30-day referral period and pays affiliates once they accumulate $50 in commissions. Those terms illustrate a desire for mutually beneficial outcomes.

Trust: Promote trustworthy products and services that are proven market winners. These goods have many legit and honest positive customer reviews on Amazon, Trustpilot, Google, and other review websites.

Content: Create unique, high-quality content that your audience will love. Also, publish content for different parts of the marketing and sales funnel, such as the top of the funnel, middle of the funnel, and bottom of the funnel. We'll cover this in more depth later.

Traffic: Get enough traffic and clicks to your site or platform and on your affiliate links, for example, a minimum of 10,000 clicks monthly. Add links, calls-to-action, banners, and other marketing materials to entice users.

Performance: Review your results monthly to identify profitable and high-potential merchants. Then, create more content about them. Next, contact them to strengthen your relationship and investigate promotional opportunities, for example, sponsored content for your website.

Image: storyset on Freepik.com

A Day in the Life of an Affiliate Marketer

A day in the life of an affiliate marketer can vary depending on individual preferences, work style, and the specific projects they are managing. However, here is a general overview of what a typical day for an affiliate marketer might involve:

Morning Routine and Planning: Affiliate marketers start their day by reviewing their goals, priorities, and tasks. They may check emails, respond to urgent messages, and plan their schedules accordingly.

Content Creation: Creating valuable content is a core aspect of affiliate marketing. This may involve writing blog posts, recording videos, or producing podcasts that provide helpful information, product reviews, or promotional content related to their chosen niche.

Content Promotion and Optimization: Once the content is created, affiliate marketers promote it to their target audience. They may utilize various channels such as social media platforms, email marketing, search engine optimization techniques, or paid advertising to drive traffic to their content and affiliate links.

Affiliate Partnership Management: Affiliate marketers often work closely with their affiliate partners, managing relationships and ensuring the smooth integration of affiliate links or banners into their content. This may involve communicating with affiliate managers, negotiating commission rates, and monitoring performance metrics.

Research and Analysis: Affiliate marketers regularly conduct market research, competitive analysis, and keyword research to identify trends, optimize their content strategy, and uncover new affiliate opportunities. They may also analyze data and metrics to track the performance of their campaigns and make data-driven decisions.

Relationship Building: Building a network and establishing relationships with other influencers, content creators, and industry professionals is essential for affiliate marketers. This can involve reaching out for collaborations, guest posting opportunities, or participating in online communities or forums to expand their reach and gain exposure.

Monitoring and Optimization: Affiliate marketers continually monitor the performance of their affiliate campaigns, track conversions, and analyze metrics such as click-through rates, conversion rates, and revenue generated. Based on the data, they adjust their strategies, optimize content, or experiment with new approaches to improve results.

Learning and Skill Development: Affiliate marketing constantly evolves, so affiliate marketers dedicate time to stay updated on industry trends, marketing techniques, and new affiliate programs or platforms. This may involve reading industry blogs, attending webinars, participating in online courses, or joining affiliate marketing communities.

Administrative Tasks: Affiliate marketing also involves administrative tasks such as managing finances, tracking expenses, and maintaining records of earnings and affiliate partnerships. They may also handle legal requirements such as disclosures and compliance with affiliate marketing regulations.

Networking and Engagement: Affiliate marketers engage with their audience by responding to comments, engaging in conversations on social media, or participating in online communities. They actively build their brand and establish themselves as trusted authorities within their niche.

The above tasks can vary depending on the affiliate marketer's focus, niche, and experience level. Some affiliate marketers may outsource certain tasks or work with a team to handle specific aspects of their affiliate marketing business.

<Chapter 3>

AFFILIATE MARKETING STEP-BY-STEP

Some people begin their affiliate marketing endeavors by wasting hundreds to thousands on fluffy online courses taught by self-proclaimed "gurus" who overpromise and underdeliver. However, there's no magic shortcut to affiliate marketing riches. Instead, we review how to get started in affiliate marketing in this chapter. Then, we cover choosing a niche and considerations.

Getting Started

Getting started in affiliate marketing involves several steps. Here's a general roadmap to help you begin your journey:

Choose Your Niche: Select a niche that aligns with your interests, expertise, and target audience. Focusing on a specific market category allows you to establish yourself as an authority and tailor your marketing efforts effectively.

Select an Affiliate Profile: Affiliates have various content and platform options, for example, a blog, YouTube channel, or landing page. We cover affiliate profiles in an upcoming chapter.

Create Compelling Content: Produce high-quality content that educates, informs, and persuades your audience to act. This can include product reviews, tutorials, comparisons, buying guides, and engaging storytelling. Content will help you establish an online platform to promote affiliate products or services.

Research Affiliate Programs: Explore different affiliate programs within your chosen niche. Look for programs that offer products or services relevant to your target audience, have a good commission structure, provide marketing resources, and have a good reputation. Popular affiliate networks like ShareASale, FlexOffers, CJ Affiliate, and Impact offer thousands of affiliate programs.

Promote Affiliate Products: Start promoting the affiliate products or services by integrating your unique affiliate links within your content. Be transparent and disclose your affiliate relationships to maintain trust with your audience.

Drive Targeted Traffic: Implement strategies to drive targeted traffic to your online platform. This can include optimizing your content for search engines, utilizing social media marketing, leveraging email marketing, running paid advertising campaigns, or collaborating with influencers or other websites in your niche.

Track and Optimize Performance: Monitor the performance of your affiliate marketing campaigns. Use analytics tools to track traffic, conversions, and sales. Analyze the data to identify areas of improvement, optimize your strategies, and make data-driven decisions to increase your conversions and earnings.

Stay Updated and Evolve: The digital marketing landscape is constantly evolving. Stay updated with industry trends, new affiliate programs, and emerging marketing strategies. Continuously learn and refine your skills to adapt to changing market conditions and maximize your success as an affiliate marketer. Most of the resources and content that can support your activities is free of charge on the internet.

We'll explore these steps in greater detail throughout the book, starting with how to choose a niche.

What Is a Niche?

In affiliate marketing, a niche refers to a specific segment or subset of a larger market. It is a distinct and specialized area of focus within an industry or topic. Instead of targeting a broad audience, niche marketing involves narrowing your target audience to a specific group with shared interests, needs, or characteristics.

Choosing a niche allows you to focus your efforts and become an authority in a specific area. By catering to a particular audience, you can create content and promote products or services that are highly relevant and valuable to that specific group. This targeted approach increases your chances of connecting with your audience, building trust, and driving conversions.

Here are a few examples to illustrate the concept of a niche:

Health and Fitness: Rather than targeting the broad health and fitness market, you might choose a niche like "keto diet for beginners," focusing specifically on providing information, resources, and product recommendations for individuals interested in adopting a ketogenic diet.

Outdoor Gear: Instead of a generic outdoor gear market, you could narrow down to a niche like "hiking and camping gear for families," tailoring your content and recommendations to families who enjoy outdoor activities together.

Personal Finance: Rather than covering personal finance, you could specialize in a niche like "investment strategies for millennials," providing insights, tips, and affiliate links to financial products or services relevant to that demographic.

By selecting a niche, you can differentiate yourself from broader competitors and establish yourself as an expert within a specific area. It allows you to tailor your content, marketing messages, and product recommendations to a defined target audience, increasing the likelihood of attracting and engaging with the right people.

Choosing a Niche & Considerations

Choosing a niche for your affiliate marketing efforts requires careful consideration and research. Here are some steps to help you choose a niche:

Identify Your Interests and Passions: Start by brainstorming your interests, hobbies, and areas of expertise. Selecting a niche that aligns with your passions can make the process more enjoyable and sustainable in the long run.

Explore Affiliate Network Categories: Top-rated affiliate networks like Impact, CJ Affiliate, and ShareASale list 30+ product/service categories, for example, accessories, automotive, B2B, clothes, financial, legal, marketing, software, travel, web hosting, etc. You can explore the available categories and subcategories to support your niche selection.

Research Market Demand: Evaluate different niches' market demand and potential profitability. Use keyword research tools (e.g., Google Keyword Planner, Semrush, and Google Trends) to identify popular search terms and gauge interest in specific topics.

Assess Competition: Analyze the competition within potential niches. Look at other affiliate marketers or websites that target similar audiences. Consider the number of existing competitors and their level of authority. While some competition is healthy, entering a highly saturated niche with dominant players might make it challenging to gain visibility and traction. Lastly, examine search engine results to evaluate how you might rank for specific topics and keywords.

Target a Specific Audience: Determine the specific audience you want to serve within your chosen niche. Consider their demographics, interests, needs, and pain points. Narrowing down your target audience helps you create targeted and tailored content that resonates with them.

Monetization Potential: Evaluate the monetization potential of the niche. Research affiliate programs, products, or services relevant to your niche and assess their commission rates, conversion potential, and availability of affiliate marketing opportunities. Ensure there are enough products or services that you can promote to earn a sustainable income.

Consider Evergreen vs. Trending Niches: Decide whether you want to focus on evergreen or trending niches. Evergreen niches are timeless and have consistent demand over time (e.g., health and wellness, personal finance, and travel). Trending niches offer opportunities for short-term success but may also have a shorter lifespan.

Evaluate Long-Term Potential: Consider the long-term potential of the niche. Will it allow you to expand, diversify, or pivot your affiliate marketing efforts in the future? Assess whether the niche has room for growth and adaptation as the market evolves.

Validate Your Niche: Validate your niche by conducting audience research and engagement. Engage with potential target audience members through social media, forums, or surveys to understand their needs, challenges, and preferences. This feedback can help you refine your niche selection and ensure there is a demand for your content and affiliate recommendations.

Remember, choosing a niche is a critical decision, and it's okay to take time to find the right fit. Be willing to experiment and adjust as you learn more about your audience and market dynamics. Finally, selecting a niche that combines your passion, market demand, and monetization potential increases your chances of building a successful affiliate marketing business.

<Chapter 4>

AFFILIATE MARKETING PROFILES

Affiliate marketing offers many avenues to generate revenue. Also, affiliates can earn multiple income streams, depending on their approach.

In this chapter, we explore affiliate profiles and platforms, how to promote links, and affiliate marketing tools.

Affiliate Profiles & Platforms

Affiliates can belong to one or multiple profiles to scale their revenues, including the following:

Blogger

A blogger creates and publishes content on a blog. A blog, short for "weblog," is an online platform where individuals or organizations share their thoughts, opinions, experiences, or information on various topics. Bloggers use written, visual, or multimedia content to engage with their audience and express their ideas.

Blogging has become a popular form of self-expression, journalism, and content marketing. Bloggers often specialize in specific niches and build a loyal following of readers interested in their expertise or content. They may cover various topics such as travel, fashion, food, technology, personal development, health, or any other subject that aligns with their interests and target audience.

Bloggers typically create blog posts regularly, from short updates to in-depth articles. They may also incorporate images, videos, infographics, and other media to enhance their content. Blogs often allow readers to leave comments, fostering interaction and discussion between the blogger and their readers.

With the growth of the internet and social media, blogging has evolved into a diverse field. Some bloggers focus on personal blogging, sharing their experiences, opinions, and stories. Others pursue professional blogging, aiming to monetize their blogs through various means, including advertising, sponsored content, affiliate marketing, or selling digital products or services.

Successful bloggers often establish themselves as trusted authorities or influencers in their respective niches, attracting a dedicated readership and potentially partnering with brands or businesses for collaborations or endorsements.

Whether as a hobby or a profession, blogging allows individuals to share their perspectives, connect with like-minded individuals, and contribute to online communities. It provides a platform for creativity, self-expression, and dissemination of valuable information and ideas.

YouTuber

A YouTuber is an individual who creates and uploads video content on the popular online video-sharing platform YouTube. YouTube has become a global platform where people can express themselves, share their talents, entertain, educate, and connect with audiences worldwide.

YouTubers produce a wide range of content, including vlogs (video blogs), tutorials, reviews, comedy sketches, music covers, gaming videos, travel documentaries, cooking demonstrations, and more. They leverage their creativity, skills, and personalities to engage with their audience and build a subscriber base.

The content on YouTube can vary greatly depending on the YouTuber's interests, expertise, and target audience. Some YouTubers focus on a specific niche or topic, while others have a more general approach. Successful YouTubers often have a unique style, distinctive brand, and consistent presence on the platform.

YouTube provides various opportunities for YouTubers to monetize their channels and earn income. This can include advertising revenue through the YouTube Partner Program, brand collaborations and sponsorships, merchandise sales, crowdfunding, and even hosting live events or shows.

Building a successful YouTube channel requires consistent content creation, audience engagement, and an understanding of the platform's algorithms and best practices. YouTubers often interact with their viewers through comments, live chats, and social media platforms to foster community and connection.

With millions of active users and an extensive range of content, YouTube has become a platform where individuals can showcase their creativity, share their passions, and turn their channel into a full-time career. However, building a successful YouTube channel typically requires time, effort, dedication, and the ability to adapt to evolving trends and audience preferences.

Social Media Marketer

A social media marketer specializes in creating, implementing, and managing marketing strategies and campaigns on various social media platforms. They leverage social media to promote brands, products, services, or content and engage with target audiences to drive awareness, engagement, and conversions.

Social media marketers are crucial in helping businesses establish a solid online presence, build brand awareness, and foster customer loyalty. They utilize the power of social media platforms such as Facebook, Instagram, Twitter, LinkedIn, YouTube, Pinterest, and others to reach and connect with their target audience effectively.

Successful social media marketers possess strong communication skills, creativity, analytical thinking, and a deep understanding of their target audience and the platforms they operate on. They have a strategic mindset, staying ahead of industry trends and leveraging social media's evolving landscape to drive meaningful business results.

Influencer

An influencer has established credibility, authority, and a significant following in a specific niche or industry. They leverage their expertise, personality, or creative content to influence their followers' opinions, behaviors, and purchasing decisions. Influencers have a strong presence on social media platforms, where they share content and engage with their audience.

Influencer marketing has become an essential component of many brands' marketing strategies. Businesses recognize the influence and reach that influencers have over their followers. Collaborating with influencers allows brands to tap into their engaged following, boost brand awareness, and drive sales or conversions.

Influencers specialize in a particular niche or industry, such as fashion, beauty, fitness, travel, technology, parenting, or any other area of interest. They have in-depth knowledge, experience, and passion for their niche, positioning themselves as trusted authorities and resources for their followers.

Influencers create high-quality and engaging content that resonates with their target audience. This may include photos, videos, blog posts, tutorials, reviews, stories, or live streams. They aim to provide valuable information, inspiration, entertainment, or solutions to their followers, often showcasing products, services, or experiences relevant to their niche.

Influencers prioritize authenticity and transparency in their interactions with their followers. They strive to build trust by being genuine, relatable, and honest about their opinions and experiences. Influencers often share personal stories, behind-the-scenes glimpses, or authentic product recommendations, fostering a deeper connection with their audience.

Influencers often collaborate with brands and businesses for sponsored content or partnerships. They may promote products or services to their audience through branded posts, product reviews, sponsored videos, or influencer campaigns. Successful influencers balance their authenticity and the brand's messaging to ensure a genuine connection with their followers.

Email Marketer

An email marketer specializes in utilizing email as a marketing tool to engage with an audience, build relationships, and drive desired actions. Their primary responsibility is creating, implementing, and managing email marketing campaigns.

Email marketers manage and grow email subscriber lists, employing various techniques to attract and retain new subscribers. They segment the email list based on demographics, interests, purchase history, or engagement level to send targeted and personalized messages.

Content creation is a significant aspect of email marketing. Email marketers create compelling and engaging content, including well-crafted copy, visually appealing templates, and personalized elements. They understand the importance of grabbing recipients' attention and inspiring them to act.

Automation is a valuable tool in the email marketer's arsenal. They leverage automation tools and techniques to send targeted and timely emails based on user behavior, triggers, or specific events. This allows for personalization and ensures subscribers receive relevant content when it matters most.

Testing and optimization are critical components of successful email marketing campaigns. Email marketers conduct A/B testing on various elements of their emails, such as subject lines, layouts, calls-to-action, and send times. By analyzing the performance metrics, such as open rates, click-through rates, conversions, and unsubscribe rates, they refine their strategies and optimize future campaigns for better results.

Compliance and data privacy are essential considerations for email marketers. They ensure their email campaigns comply with relevant data protection regulations, such as GDPR or CAN-SPAM Act, and respect subscribers' privacy rights. Managing opt-ins, unsubscribe requests, and data security is crucial in maintaining trust with the audience.

Analytics and reporting play a vital role in evaluating the success of email campaigns. Email marketers use software and analytics tools to track and measure performance metrics. This helps them assess the effectiveness of their campaigns, make data-driven decisions, and identify areas for improvement.

Internet or Pay-Per-Click (PPC) Marketer

Internet marketer is a catchall term for people who spend most of their time promoting physical or digital products and services online. They use one or multiple digital marketing strategies to generate revenue.

A typical internet marketing strategy is to drive traffic to a landing page featuring an introductory video. Next, the internet marketer encourages the user to enter her email address for more information regarding a course, tutorial, or webinar.

While some internet marketers focus on organic traffic, many pay for traffic by running ads on search engines and social media websites like Facebook.

Coupon/Deal Site Owner

A coupon website is an online platform that aggregates and provides a collection of discount codes, promotional offers, and coupons from various retailers and brands. These websites aim to help consumers save money by providing easy access to discounts and deals for online and offline purchases.

The primary function of a coupon website is to gather and organize coupons from different sources, such as retailers, brands, and affiliate programs. Coupon websites may partner directly with businesses to offer exclusive deals to their users. They typically categorize coupons based on product categories, brands, or retailers to facilitate user navigation and search.

Coupon websites are a valuable resource for consumers looking to find discounts and save money on purchases. Users can visit these websites, search for specific products or brands, and find coupons or promotional codes available. They can then apply these codes during the checkout process on the retailer's website.

Coupon websites strive to keep their coupon database up to date by regularly adding new coupons, removing expired ones, and notifying users about the latest deals and offers.

Some coupon websites provide user-generated reviews and ratings for coupons, helping users make informed decisions and avoid coupons that may not work as expected.

Coupon websites often utilize affiliate marketing, earning a commission for each sale made through their website. This allows them to provide free coupon access while generating revenue through affiliate partnerships.

Loyalty/Reward Site Owner

A loyalty website, also known as a rewards or loyalty program website, is an online platform that allows businesses to implement and manage customer loyalty programs. These programs are designed to encourage customer retention, engagement, and repeat purchases by offering rewards, incentives, and exclusive benefits to loyal customers.

The primary function of a loyalty website is to provide a central hub where customers can sign up, track their loyalty program status, earn points, redeem rewards, and access program-related information. It serves as a platform for businesses to communicate with their loyal customers and provide a seamless experience for managing and enjoying the loyalty program's benefits.

Loyalty websites allow customers to easily enroll in the loyalty program by creating an account or linking it to their existing customer account. They may provide incentives, such as welcome bonuses or exclusive discounts, to encourage customers to join.

Once enrolled, customers can earn points for various actions, such as making purchases, referring friends, engaging with the brand on social media, or completing specific activities determined by the loyalty program. The loyalty website tracks and displays the customers' points balance.

Customers can use their accumulated points to redeem rewards the loyalty program offers. Loyalty websites provide a catalog of rewards, including discounts, free products, exclusive access to events, personalized recommendations, or other incentives.

Online Course Instructor

An online course instructor leads and facilitates learning in an online educational setting. They are responsible for designing, developing, and delivering course content to students through digital platforms. Online course instructors are pivotal in guiding students' learning journeys, providing essential knowledge, and fostering a supportive and interactive learning environment. They may use various tools such as video lectures, discussion forums, quizzes, and assignments to engage students and assess their progress.

Online course instructors often provide feedback and support to students, answering questions, addressing concerns, and encouraging active participation to ensure a successful learning experience for all participants.

eBook Author

An ebook author writes and publishes an electronic book (ebook). Ebooks can be read on various devices, including computers, tablets, and smartphones. Ebook authors can self-publish their work or work with a traditional publisher. Amazon's Kindle Direct Publishing is a leading platform for self-publishing books. Authors can add affiliate links to their ebooks.

Podcaster

A podcaster creates, hosts, and publishes audio content as podcasts. A podcast is a digital audio file series that listeners can subscribe to and download or stream from the internet. Podcasting has gained immense popularity as a medium for sharing information, entertainment, storytelling, and discussions on various topics.

Podcasters are responsible for conceptualizing, producing, and distributing their podcast episodes. They typically have a specific theme, niche, or subject matter that they focus on, catering to a particular target audience. Podcasters often use their unique voice, expertise, or storytelling skills to engage and connect with their listeners.

Website Owner

Regardless of the industry, some website owners participate in affiliate marketing. For example, a dog clothing company uses its blog to promote related dog products.

Image: pikisuperstar on Freepik.com

How to Promote Affiliate Links

Affiliate marketing requires adding links to digital content and webpages, for example, blog posts and email campaigns. Let's review how each affiliate profile can distribute links.

Bloggers can add affiliate links and media assets like banners to their articles, widgets, images, comments, and menus.

YouTubers can add links to their video descriptions, comments, posts, and about page links.

Social media marketers can add links to posts, bios, and direct messages. Also, many social media marketers use link landing pages like Linktree and Bitly to feature multiple links.

Influencers and website owners can promote links the same way as bloggers, YouTubers, and social media marketers.

Email marketers can add links to their newsletters and email signatures.

Internet, performance, and webinar marketers can add links to their landing pages, content, and paid ads (if the merchant allows it).

Online course instructors can promote links in their content, descriptions, resources, and comments.

eBook authors can add links to their manuscripts.

Coupon/deal sites can promote links in their content and images.

Loyalty/reward sites can promote links in their content and images.

Podcasters can promote links in their episode descriptions, show notes, and on their associated digital assets like websites and email newsletters. Podcasters like YouTubers can and should instruct their listeners and viewers on where to go for links, for example, "You'll find the link in my description" or "Visit www.websitename.com/resources for a special discount."

Deep Linking

Deep linking is a technique used in affiliate marketing to create hyperlinks that direct users to a specific page or content on a merchant's site, rather than the homepage or a generic landing page. It allows affiliates to send users directly to the most relevant and specific content related to their product or promotion.

With deep linking, affiliates can bypass general product listings and instead direct users to a specific product page, category page, blog post, or any other targeted content within the merchant's website. This helps to improve user experience by delivering them directly to the information or product they are interested in, increasing the likelihood of conversion.

Deep linking is achieved by appending additional parameters to the standard affiliate link. These parameters typically include the URL of the page or content the affiliate wants to direct the user to. Users who click on a deep link are taken directly to the specified page rather than the default landing page.

Benefits of deep linking in affiliate marketing include:

Enhanced User Experience: Deep linking ensures that users are directed to the most relevant content, improving their overall experience and reducing the number of clicks required to find what they seek.

Increased Conversion Rates: By guiding users to specific pages related to the promotion or product being promoted, deep linking can increase the chances of conversions and sales. Users are more likely to complete a purchase when they land on a page that matches their intent.

Targeted Marketing: Deep linking allows affiliates to target specific audience segments with personalized and relevant content. By directing users to specific pages or products, affiliates can tailor their marketing messages and promotions for better engagement and conversions.

Better Tracking and Analytics: Deep linking enables more granular tracking and analytics, as affiliates can track clicks and conversions for specific pages or products. This allows for a more precise analysis of campaign performance and optimization.

Deep linking is especially useful when promoting individual products, specific promotions, or targeted content within a merchant's website. It helps affiliates deliver a seamless user experience, increase engagement, and improve the likelihood of earning commissions through leads and sales.

Affiliate Marketing Tools

Affiliate marketers utilize various tools and resources to streamline workflow, optimize strategies, and track performance. Here are some standard tools used by affiliate marketers:

Website/Blog: A website or blog is often the central hub for affiliate marketing activities. It allows affiliates to create content, publish reviews, and showcase affiliate links. Content management systems like WordPress are popular for building and managing affiliate websites.

Keyword Research Tools: Tools like Google Keyword Planner, Google Trends, and Semrush help affiliate marketers identify relevant keywords and search terms to optimize their content for better search engine rankings and targeted traffic.

SEO Tools: SEO tools like Moz, Yoast SEO, or SE Ranking help affiliates optimize their websites for search engines, conduct competitor research, and track keyword rankings.

Content Creation & Writing Tools: Tools like Grammarly, Hemingway Editor, or CoSchedule Headline Analyzer help affiliates create high-quality content, improve readability, and optimize headlines for better engagement.

Link Cloaking/Shortening Tools: Link cloaking or shortening tools like Pretty Links, Bitly, or ThirstyAffiliates allow affiliates to create shorter, more visually appealing affiliate links. They also provide tracking and analytics features to monitor link performance.

Social Media Management Tools: Tools like Buffer, Hootsuite, and Sprout Social help affiliates schedule and manage their social media posts across multiple platforms.

They provide analytics to track social media performance and engage with the audience efficiently.

Email Marketing Tools: Email marketing apps such as GetResponse, MailerLite, and Moosend assist affiliates in building and managing their email lists, creating newsletters, and automating email campaigns to promote affiliate products.

Analytics and Tracking Tools: Google Analytics is a powerful tool to track website traffic, user behavior, and conversions. Affiliate networks and platforms often provide tracking tools and dashboards to monitor clicks, conversions, and earnings.

Affiliate Network/Platform Tools: Affiliate networks and platforms like ShareASale, CJ Affiliate, or Amazon Associates provide reporting and analytics tools to track performance, generate affiliate links, and access promotional materials.

Productivity and Organization Tools: Tools like Trello, Asana, Monday.com, Notion, and ClickUp help affiliate marketers stay organized, manage projects, and plan content creation and promotion activities.

<Chapter 5>

CONTENT, FUNNELS, & TRAFFIC

Content is the soul of affiliate marketing; affiliates have various options to delight and convert their audiences. Marketers create content to hit different stages and categories of the marketing funnel and persuade prospective customers. We'll review the topics and familiar traffic sources in this chapter.

Types of Content

Bloggers, YouTubers, social media marketers, and creators have many content options to get traffic, for example, a product review or comparison article. Additionally, the following content types can be published in different formats, including text, video, audio, or graphical.

Listicle

A listicle is an article or blog post that presents information or content as a list. The term "listicle" is a combination of the words "list" and "article." Listicles are favored in online media and are characterized by their concise and easily scannable format. They often incorporate a numbered or bulleted list to organize and present information in a digestible and engaging way.

Here are some key features of listicles:

Numerical Format: Listicles typically feature a numbered or bulleted format, such as "10 Ways to..." or "Top 5 Tips for...". Using numbers helps create a structured and sequential flow, making it easy for readers to follow along.

Concise and Snackable Content: Listicles are known for their bite-sized, easily consumable content. Each point in the list is usually brief and focused, providing critical information or insights without excessive elaboration.

Skimmable Structure: Listicles are designed to be quickly scanned and skimmed by readers. The numbered or bulleted format lets readers quickly identify the main points and decide which sections to dive deeper into.

Variety and Diversity: Listicles often incorporate a variety of items, ideas, or examples within the list. They may include different perspectives, options, or examples to provide a comprehensive view of a topic or offer a range of suggestions.

Engaging Titles: Listicles often have catchy and attention-grabbing titles that highlight the number of items in the list and create curiosity or interest. Titles like "10 Must-Try Recipes" or "7 Surprising Facts About..." entice readers to click and explore the content.

Visual Elements: Listicles often include visual elements, such as images, gifs, or infographics, to enhance the presentation and make the content visually appealing. Visuals help break up the text and provide additional context or illustration.

Shareability: Listicles are highly shareable content due to their easily digestible format and appealing titles. Readers often find them interesting and enjoyable to read and are likelier to share them on social media platforms or with their peers.

Listicles are popular because they offer a structured and engaging way to present information, making complex topics more accessible and entertaining. They cater to readers' preferences for quick content consumption in an era with shorter attention spans. Listicles have become a standard format across various online platforms, including news websites, blogs, and social media, providing a balance of information and entertainment.

How-to, Tutorial, or Guide

How-to articles, instructional articles, or tutorials provide step-by-step instructions and guidance on accomplishing a specific task or learning a new skill. These articles aim to educate readers by breaking down complex processes into manageable steps, making them easy to follow and implement.

How-to articles have these standard features:

Clear Objective: How-to articles have a specific objective or outcome in mind. They focus on teaching readers how to do something, whether it's a practical task like fixing a leaky faucet, a creative skill like painting a landscape, or a digital skill like coding a website.

Step-by-Step Instructions: How-to articles provide a structured sequence of steps readers can follow to achieve the desired outcome. Each step is typically explained in detail, outlining the necessary actions, tools, or materials.

Descriptive Language: These articles use clear and concise language to ensure readers understand and execute each step efficiently. They avoid jargon or technical terms unless necessary and may include definitions or explanations for unfamiliar words.

Visual Aids: How-to articles often incorporate visual aids, such as images, diagrams, or videos, to enhance understanding and provide visual guidance. Visuals can clarify complex concepts, illustrate specific actions, or showcase results.

Relevant Examples: Some how-to articles include examples or case studies to illustrate different scenarios or approaches. These examples help readers apply the instructions to their situations and adapt them as needed.

Troubleshooting and FAQs: In many cases, how-to articles address common issues or challenges readers may encounter during the process. They may include troubleshooting tips, FAQs, or workarounds to help readers overcome obstacles and succeed.

Formatting and Organization: How-to articles often use clear headings, subheadings, and bullet points to organize the content and make it scannable. This formatting makes it easier for readers to locate specific steps or revisit sections as needed.

Call-to-Action: Some how-to articles conclude with a call-to-action, encouraging readers to act and apply what they have learned. This can include suggestions for further practice, additional resources, or recommendations for related topics.

Product or Service Comparison

A product comparison article (or video) compares multiple products or services within a specific category or industry. These articles aim to help consumers make informed purchasing decisions by comprehensively analyzing the features, benefits, pricing, and other relevant factors of different products.

Product comparison articles typically include the following elements:

Introduction: The report begins with an introduction that sets the context and explains the purpose of the comparison. It may outline the criteria used for evaluation and emphasize the importance of making an informed choice.

Product Selection: The article identifies and lists the products being compared, often focusing on popular or highly regarded options within the given category. The selection may include both well-known brands and emerging alternatives.

Comparative Analysis: The heart of a product comparison article lies in the detailed analysis of each product's features, specifications, performance, pricing, and other relevant factors. The article typically compares these aspects, highlighting similarities and differences between the products.

Pros and Cons: A product comparison article explores the strengths and weaknesses of each product. It objectively presents the advantages and disadvantages of using a particular product, helping readers understand the trade-offs associated with each option.

User Reviews and Ratings: Product comparison articles often incorporate user reviews and ratings from reputable sources to provide a well-rounded perspective. These insights offer real-world experiences and opinions from consumers who have used the products.

Pricing and Value: The article considers the pricing of each product and evaluates the features and benefits provided. It helps readers assess the value for money and make decisions based on their budget and preferences.

Recommendation or Conclusion: A product comparison article may provide advice or a conclusion based on the comparative analysis. This can summarize the article's findings, highlighting the product that best suits specific needs or offering a ranking of the products based on their performance.

Additional Resources: Some product comparison articles may include other resources, such as links to in-depth reviews, buying guides, or related articles. These resources provide readers with further information to support their decision-making process.

Product or Service Review

A product review article is content that provides an in-depth evaluation and assessment of a specific product or service. These articles aim to provide readers with detailed information, insights, and opinions about a product's features, performance, usability, and overall value.

Here are the critical items usually found in a product review article:

Introduction: The article begins with an introduction that sets the context and introduces the reviewed product. It may include a brief overview of the product's purpose, target audience, or market segment.

Product Description: The article provides a comprehensive description of the product, including its specifications, design, dimensions, materials used, and any notable features or functionalities.

Testing and Evaluation: The reviewer shares their firsthand experience with the product. This may involve using the product extensively, testing its various features and capabilities, and assessing its performance in real-world scenarios.

Pros and Cons: The article presents the advantages and disadvantages of the product. It objectively highlights the strengths and benefits it offers and any limitations or drawbacks that users should be aware of.

User-Focused Assessment: A product review article often analyzes how well the product meets the needs and expectations of its intended users. It considers factors such as ease of use, durability, reliability, and user-friendliness.

Comparisons: Product review articles may sometimes compare the reviewed product with similar or competing products. This gives readers a frame of reference and helps them understand the product's positioning and competitive advantages.

Performance and Functionality: The article dives into the product's performance in different aspects, such as speed, accuracy, efficiency, or effectiveness. It evaluates how well the product delivers its intended purpose or solves the problems it claims to address.

Visuals and Media: Product review articles often include visuals, such as images or videos, to supplement the text and provide readers with a visual representation of the product. These visuals may showcase the product's design, interface, or usage in action.

Verdict or Recommendation: Based on the evaluation, the article concludes with a judgment or recommendation about the product. This can summarize the reviewer's overall assessment and whether they recommend the product to potential buyers.

Disclosure: Ethical product review articles often include a disclosure statement indicating any potential conflicts of interest, affiliations, or sponsorships that may impact the objectivity of the review.

Product or Service Alternatives

A product alternatives article is a type of content that presents a list of alternative products or services as substitutes or options to consider instead of a particular product. These articles aim to provide readers with various choices and expand their options when making purchasing decisions.

In addition to content elements for product comparisons and reviews, alternative product content includes the following:

Criteria for Alternatives: The article establishes the standards or factors on which the alternatives are based. These criteria may include price, features, functionality, brand reputation, customer reviews, or any specific requirements that readers may have.

List of Alternatives: The article's core is the list of alternative products or services. Each alternative is presented with a brief description, including its key features, benefits, and how it compares to the original product.

Comparison Chart or Table: In some cases, a product alternatives article may include a comparison chart or table highlighting the key differences and similarities among the alternatives. This can help readers make quick comparisons and assess which option may be most suitable for their needs.

Trending & What's Hot

Trending content often covers current events, emerging topics, breaking news, or subjects of widespread interest. They provide fresh perspectives or timely insights that capture the attention of readers and viewers.

Trending content presents unique ideas, fresh viewpoints, or innovative concepts that generate interest and stand out. They offer a novel take on a subject or provide new information that has yet to be widely known.

Interview

Interview content refers to articles, videos, podcasts, or any form of media that feature interviews with individuals or groups. It involves a conversation or discussion between an interviewer and one or more interviewees to obtain insights, information, or perspectives on a particular topic.

Interview content can take various forms, including:

Written Interviews: These are traditional interview articles where the questions and answers are presented in a written format. They may be conducted in person, over the phone, via email, or other communication channels.

Video Interviews: Video interviews involve recording the conversation between the interviewer and interviewee(s). They provide a visual element and allow viewers to observe facial expressions, body language, and other non-verbal cues.

Podcast Interviews: Podcast interviews are audio recordings where the interviewer converses with the interviewee(s). They are typically released as episodes within a podcast series.

Panel Discussions: Panel discussions bring together multiple experts or individuals with diverse viewpoints to discuss a specific topic. The moderator guides the conversation, and the panelists share their insights and opinions.

Q&A Sessions: Question-and-answer sessions involve the audience or readers submitting questions and the interviewee(s) responding to those questions. This format allows for direct engagement with the interviewee(s) and can provide tailored information based on audience interests.

Interview content offers several benefits, such as:

Expert Insights: Interviews provide an opportunity to tap into the knowledge and expertise of industry leaders, professionals, or individuals with specific experiences. They can offer unique perspectives, valuable advice, or insider information on a particular subject.

Credibility and Trust: Interview content featuring respected experts or influential individuals can enhance the credibility and trustworthiness of the information presented. It adds authority and expertise to the topic being discussed.

Engagement and Variety: Interviews can engage audiences as they involve a dynamic conversation rather than a one-sided presentation. They add variety to content offerings, catering to different preferences and learning styles.

Human Connection: Interview content allows readers, viewers, or listeners to connect with the interviewee(s) more personally. It humanizes the content and creates a sense of relatability and authenticity.

Storytelling Opportunities: Interviews often provide a platform for individuals to share personal stories, experiences, or anecdotes that can inspire, educate, or entertain the audience. This storytelling aspect can make the content more captivating and memorable.

Unboxing

Unboxing content refers to videos or articles that document unpacking and revealing the contents of a newly purchased or received product. Unboxing videos have gained significant popularity, particularly on platforms like YouTube, where creators film themselves, opening product packaging and sharing their initial impressions.

Unboxing content can serve various purposes, such as providing product reviews, showcasing new releases, generating excitement around a brand, or simply offering entertainment to viewers who enjoy the anticipation and discovery involved in the unboxing experience. It can be particularly influential for consumers who rely on these videos to make informed purchasing decisions or gain insights into the features and quality of products before making a buying choice.

Here are some critical aspects of unboxing content:

Visual Experience: Unboxing content is primarily visual, as it allows viewers to see the packaging, materials, and components of a product firsthand. Creators often focus on providing clear shots of the unboxing process, showcasing the packaging design, labels, and any included accessories.

Initial Reactions and Impressions: Unboxing content captures the creator's genuine and immediate reactions to the product. They may share their initial thoughts, excitement, or surprise as they explore the contents of the package. This adds an element of authenticity and relatability for viewers.

Product Presentation: Unboxing videos often showcase the product, highlighting its design, features, and functionality. Creators may demonstrate how to assemble or set up the product and discuss its critical attributes while providing commentary or explanations.

Comparisons and Specifications: In some cases, unboxing content may include comparisons with similar products or previous models. Creators may highlight unboxing products' differences, improvements, or unique selling points.

User Experience: Unboxing content may touch upon the creator's first impressions of the product, including factors like build quality, ergonomics, user interface, or any initial challenges encountered during setup or operation.

Packaging Analysis: Unboxing content often pays attention to the packaging itself, examining its aesthetics, durability, branding, and any additional information or promotional materials included. Creators may discuss the packaging's functionality and assess its overall appeal.

Viewer Engagement: Unboxing content invites viewer engagement by encouraging comments, questions, or feedback about the unboxed product or related topics. Creators may ask for viewer opinions or invite discussions on specific aspects of the product.

Case Study

Case study content is a form of content that presents an in-depth analysis and examination of a specific real-world situation, problem, or scenario. It involves studying a particular case or example to understand its context, identify challenges, analyze strategies or solutions, and draw insights or lessons from the experience. The case study content is widely used in business, marketing, psychology, healthcare, and social sciences.

Here are the key elements typically found in case study content:

Introduction: The case study begins with an introduction that sets the stage by providing background information about the subject of the case study. This includes details about the industry, company, organization, or individuals involved.

Objectives: The case study outlines the objectives or goals of the study. This helps readers understand the purpose and focus of the analysis and what specific aspects will be examined.

Problem or Challenge: The case study presents the problem or challenge faced by the subject of the study. It outlines the issues, obstacles, or complexities that need to be addressed and clearly explains the context.

Methodology: The case study describes the methods or approach used to gather information and analyze. This may involve interviews, surveys, data collection, observations, or qualitative and quantitative research methods.

Analysis and Findings: The case study presents a detailed analysis of the problem, strategies, tactics, or solutions employed, and their outcomes. It highlights the essential findings and insights from examining the case, including successes, failures, lessons learned, and relevant data or evidence.

Discussion and Interpretation: The case study provides a discussion and interpretation of the findings. It explores the case study's implications, significance, and broader applications, connecting it to relevant theories, concepts, or industry practices.

Recommendations: Based on the analysis and findings, the case study may offer suggestions for addressing challenges or improving outcomes in similar situations. These recommendations should be practical and actionable.

Visuals and Examples: Case study content often includes visuals, such as charts, graphs, diagrams, or real-life examples, to support the analysis and provide visual representations of data or concepts.

Conclusion: The case study concludes by summarizing the main points, reiterating the key insights or lessons learned, and highlighting any future implications or areas for further research.

Company or Market Research

Company or market research content refers to content that focuses on analyzing and providing insights into specific companies, industries, or market trends. It involves conducting thorough research and collecting data to present informative and valuable content to readers or target audiences. This type of content aims to help individuals or businesses make informed decisions, understand market dynamics, identify opportunities, and stay updated on industry developments.

Company or market research content usually includes the following items:

Company Profiles: Research content may include in-depth profiles of companies, providing information about their history, mission, products or services, market position, financial performance, competitive landscape, and key executives. These profiles help readers gain a comprehensive understanding of a particular company and its operations.

Industry Analysis: Market research content often involves analyzing specific industries or sectors. It may include evaluating the market size, growth rates, industry trends, challenges, and key players. Industry analysis content provides readers with a broader view of the market landscape and helps them understand the dynamics that impact businesses within that industry.

Market Reports and Surveys: Research content can include market reports or survey results that provide statistical data, insights, and forecasts related to specific markets, consumer behavior, or industry trends. These reports help readers gauge market potential, identify consumer preferences, and make informed business decisions.

Competitive Analysis: Research content may focus on comparing and analyzing competitors within a particular industry. It may include assessing strengths, weaknesses, market positioning, product offerings, pricing strategies, and marketing tactics of competing companies. Competitive analysis content helps readers understand the competitive landscape and make strategic decisions accordingly.

Trend Analysis: Research content often explores emerging trends, technological advancements, or shifts in consumer behavior that impact specific industries or markets. This content aims to give readers insights into upcoming opportunities or challenges and helps them stay ahead of the curve.

Data Interpretation and Visualization: Market research content often involves analyzing and interpreting data collected from various sources such as surveys, market studies, or industry reports. It may present data in charts, graphs, infographics, or visualizations to make it more accessible and understandable to readers.

Thought Leadership and Expert Opinions: Research content may feature expert opinions, thought leadership pieces, or interviews with industry professionals. These insights give readers valuable perspectives, specialist advice, or predictions based on their experience and knowledge in a particular field.

Targeted Audience: Market research content is typically aimed at professionals, entrepreneurs, investors, or individuals seeking information or insights about a specific industry, market, or company.

Webinar or Online Course

Webinar content refers to educational or informational content delivered through a live or pre-recorded web-based seminar, known as a webinar. Webinars are interactive online events that allow presenters to share knowledge, insights, and expertise with a virtual audience.

Webinars offer a convenient and accessible format for delivering content to a broad audience. They provide opportunities for engagement, knowledge sharing, and learning in a virtual setting. Webinar content can be used by businesses, educators, trainers, or experts as a valuable tool for disseminating information, building relationships, and promoting their expertise.

Here are some critical aspects of webinar content:

Presentation: Webinars typically involve a presenter or a panel of experts who deliver a presentation on a specific topic. The content can cover various subjects, such as industry trends, best practices, product demonstrations, case studies, or instructional sessions.

Visual Materials: Webinars often include visuals, such as slides, charts, graphs, or videos, to support the presentation and enhance the audience's understanding of the content. These visual elements help to convey information effectively and keep participants engaged.

Interactivity: Webinars provide interactive features that allow participants to engage with the presenter and ask questions in real time. This can be done through chat boxes, Q&A sessions, or polling features, enabling two-way communication between the presenter and the audience.

Collaboration and Guest Speakers: Webinars sometimes feature guest speakers or industry experts contributing their insights and perspectives. This collaboration adds variety and depth to the content and can attract a larger audience.

Recording and On-Demand Access: Webinars are often recorded, allowing participants who couldn't attend the live event to access the content at their convenience. The recorded webinars can be made available as on-demand content, extending the original webinar's reach and impact.

Training and Workshops: Webinars are commonly used to provide participants with practical knowledge and skills. They can involve interactive exercises, demonstrations, or hands-on workshops to facilitate learning and practical application of the content.

Promotional Content: Webinars can also serve as a platform for promotional purposes, such as product launches, previews, or special offers. They allow businesses to showcase their products or services and provide detailed information to potential customers.

Targeted Audience: Webinars are often tailored to a specific audience, such as professionals in a particular industry, customers of a specific product or service, or individuals with a specific interest or expertise. The content is designed to address their needs, challenges, or interests effectively.

Resources or Tools

Many affiliates have a resources or tools page highlighting the apps they use regularly. For example, a YouTuber covering personal finance links to his tools page, listing his favorite financial apps for budgeting, saving, and investing.

Book

Some affiliates write books for their audiences. For example, a food blogger can offer a short recipe book to entice people to sign up for her newsletter. Alternatively, she might publish an ebook on Amazon to promote her site and generate sales.

Deal or Coupon

Affiliates can create content concerning a deal, coupon, or sales event. Then, they can promote it on their chosen platforms, for example, with a social media post or email newsletter.

The Marketing Funnel

The marketing funnel, or the sales or purchase funnel, is a conceptual framework that illustrates the customer's journey from initial awareness of a product or service to purchasing. It represents a customer's various stages before converting into a paying customer. The marketing funnel is typically divided into several stages, each with its purpose and strategies.

The marketing funnel helps businesses understand the customer journey and tailor their efforts to each stage. By guiding potential customers through the funnel, companies can effectively nurture leads, build trust, and increase the likelihood of conversion. It also allows businesses to identify areas of improvement, optimize marketing strategies, and maximize the overall effectiveness of their marketing efforts.

The Six Marketing Funnel Stages

Awareness Stage: This is the top of the funnel, where the goal is to attract the attention of potential customers and generate awareness of your brand, product, or service. Marketing activities in this stage aim to reach a broad audience and include tactics such as content marketing, social media advertising, search engine optimization, and public relations.

Interest Stage: Once potential customers become aware of your brand, the goal is to pique their interest and engage them further. At this stage, you provide more information about your offerings, showcase the value proposition, and establish credibility. Content marketing, lead magnets (e.g., ebooks, whitepapers), webinars, and email marketing campaigns are commonly used tactics in this stage.

Consideration Stage: In this stage, potential customers actively consider your product or service and evaluate it against other options. The goal is to demonstrate how your offering solves their needs or problems. Content tactics may include case studies, product demos, testimonials, comparison guides, or free trials.

Decision Stage: At this stage, potential customers are ready to purchase. The focus is on providing incentives, addressing any concerns or objections, and making it easy for customers to complete the purchase. Tactics may include discounts, limited-time offers, customer reviews, persuasive copywriting, and seamless checkout processes.

Action Stage: This is the bottom of the funnel, where potential customers convert into paying customers by taking the desired action, such as purchasing, signing up for a subscription, or filling out a form. After the conversion, the customer becomes a part of your customer base.

Retention and Loyalty Stage: The marketing funnel continues after the initial purchase. Building customer loyalty and retaining customers is crucial for long-term success. Activities in this stage focus on providing exceptional customer service, nurturing relationships, and offering additional value to encourage repeat purchases and foster brand advocacy.

Image: vectorjuice on Freepik.com

Content for Different Stages

Marketers should diversify their content for different marketing funnel stages because they need to do so to avoid missed sales opportunities. The different stages of the marketing funnel require tailored content strategies to guide potential customers through the buying journey effectively. By providing valuable and relevant content at each stage, businesses can engage with their audience, build trust, and increase the likelihood of conversions. It's important to note that the specific types of content used may vary depending on the industry, target audience, and business marketing goals.

Here are the three content funnel categories:

Top-of-Funnel (TOFU) Content: Top-of-funnel content is designed to attract a broad audience and generate awareness of your brand or product. Its primary goal is to capture the attention of potential customers and provide them with valuable information or entertainment. TOFU content is typically educational, engaging, and focused on something other than direct sales pitches. Examples of TOFU content include blog posts, social media posts, infographics, videos, podcasts, and quizzes.

Mid-Funnel (MOFU) Content: Mid-funnel content is aimed at engaging and nurturing leads who have shown interest in your brand or product. At this stage, the goal is to provide more specific information and guide potential customers toward considering your solution a viable option. MOFU content often addresses the needs and pain points of the target audience and offers more in-depth information about your product or service. Examples of MOFU content include case studies, product guides, webinars, email newsletters, and interactive tools or calculators.

Bottom-of-Funnel (BOFU) Content: Bottom-of-funnel content is designed to convert leads into customers by providing the necessary information and incentives to make a purchase decision. The audience is typically more qualified and actively considering a purchase at this stage. BOFU content addresses objections, provides social proof, and offers incentives to encourage conversions. Examples of BOFU content include product demonstrations, free trials, customer testimonials, pricing comparisons, personalized offers, and product samples.

Traffic Sources

The most common online traffic sources refer to the channels or platforms visitors discover and access a website or online content.

Here are the six traffic sources tracked in Google Analytics, a web analytics tool provided by Google:

Organic Search refers to traffic from search engines like Google, Bing, or Yahoo. It occurs when users enter relevant keywords or phrases in a search engine and click on the organic search results.

Direct Traffic occurs when visitors directly type a website's URL into their browser or use a bookmark to access the website. It also includes traffic from untraceable sources, such as when someone manually types a URL into an email or document.

Referral Traffic is generated when visitors click on a link from another website to reach your website. This can happen through backlinks, guest posts, social media posts, online directories, or other websites linking to your content. Affiliate and influencer activities may roll up into referral traffic.

Social Media Traffic: Social media platforms like Facebook, Instagram, Twitter, LinkedIn, and YouTube can generate website traffic through shared links, posts, or advertisements. Users click on these links and are directed to the respective websites.

Paid search traffic refers to visitors who reach a website through paid advertisements on search engines and social media sites, such as Google Ads, Bing Ads, or Facebook ads. Advertisers bid on specific keywords, displaying their ads when users search for them.

Email marketing traffic can be generated through email marketing campaigns where users receive emails containing links to specific web pages or offers. When recipients click these links, they are directed to the designated web pages.

Other Traffic Sources

Display advertising involves placing graphical or banner ads on websites, blogs, or apps. When users click on these ads, they are directed to the advertiser's website, generating traffic.

Active participation in online forums, discussion boards, chat app groups, or niche-specific communities can generate traffic as users engage with your posts, profiles, or signatures containing links to your website.

Paying for Traffic

Most affiliates rely on organic traffic to drive sales. However, some affiliates pay for traffic via Google and social media ads. While some affiliates achieve profitability with paid traffic, the strategy isn't recommended for the following reasons:

- Ads Are Costly: Online advertising is getting more expensive daily, eroding profitability.
- Many Advertisers Forbid It: Many advertisers prohibit affiliates from running ads to keep their paid marketing costs low. When affiliates run ads, they bid against merchants, driving up prices.
- Merchants Don't Share Data: Most merchants won't share internal marketing and sales data with affiliates. However, that data is necessary to optimize the return on advertising spend (ROAS). For example, knowing which countries to target would help you, but merchants are unlikely to give you that information.
- Ad Network Rules: Google Ads and other platforms don't fully support redirects from third-party affiliate links. So, your account might end up getting suspended or terminated.
- Affiliate Marketing Isn't E-commerce: Millions of online retailers pay for website traffic, which makes sense because their ads take users directly to their sites. Contrastingly, third-party affiliate links bounce around URLs, making them less efficient.

<Chapter 6>

AFFILIATE SOFTWARE & PROGRAMS

Affiliate marketing wouldn't be a billion-dollar industry today without robust digital marketing software to track and attribute sales accordingly and efficiently. Reliable tracking is more critical than ever in the face of browser privacy scrutiny and user security. Additionally, affiliate marketing software has had to adapt to an expanding multichannel and device landscape to tag users across marketing funnel stages and customer journeys.

Affiliates must know where to look to join programs. First, however, they must know what to consider to ensure successful partnerships. We review affiliate marketing software, tracking methods, program considerations, and reputable affiliate networks in this chapter.

Affiliate Marketing Software

Affiliate marketers will come across three types of affiliate marketing tracking apps, including affiliate networks, affiliate marketing software, and in-house software.

Affiliate networks: These third-party platforms connect advertisers (merchants) with publishers (affiliates). Examples include ShareASale, CJ Affiliate, and Impact.

Affiliate marketing software: These standalone software solutions allow businesses to track and manage their affiliate programs. Examples include Post Affiliate Pro and LinkMink.

In-house affiliate marketing software: Some businesses develop proprietary tracking systems to manage their affiliate programs and track affiliate-generated sales or leads, such as Amazon Associates.

One benefit of affiliate marketing software over networks is using first-party links and cookies to thwart browser-blocking protocols.

Tracking Methods

Efficient tracking in affiliate and digital marketing is critical. Here are the ways affiliate marketing apps track marketing activities and conversions.

URL Tracking Parameters: This method appends unique tracking parameters to affiliate links. These parameters help track specific actions and identify the source of traffic and conversions. Commonly used parameters include UTM parameters (e.g., utm_source, utm_medium) and custom tracking variables.

Cookie-based Tracking: Cookies are small text files stored on a user's browser that store information related to their interactions with a website. Affiliate marketing programs often use cookies to track referrals and attribute commissions to the appropriate affiliate.

Pixel Tracking: Pixel tracking involves placing a tracking pixel or snippet of code on the advertiser's website. This code fires when a specific action, such as a purchase or lead submission, allows the tracking software to record the conversion.

Server-to-Server (S2S) Tracking: S2S tracking involves directly communicating tracking information between the advertiser's server and the affiliate network or tracking platform's server. This method ensures accurate and reliable monitoring without relying on browser-based tracking.

Multi-channel Attribution: This tracking method attributes conversions to multiple touchpoints along the customer journey rather than solely crediting the last click. It provides a more holistic view of each affiliate's value to the conversion process.

Affiliate Program Considerations

Sprinting to join every program in sight will not make you successful. Instead, affiliates should evaluate several factors to ensure they choose the right programs that align with their goals and maximize their earning potential. Here are some key factors to consider:

Commission Structure: Examine the commission rates offered by the affiliate program. Consider whether they offer a flat commission, a tiered commission based on performance, or a percentage of the sale. Evaluate which structure will provide the most favorable earnings for your efforts.

Product or Service Relevance: Assess the relevance of the products or services offered by the affiliate program to your target audience. The more closely aligned they are to your niche or audience's interests, the higher the likelihood of generating conversions and earning commissions.

Cookie Duration: Understand the cookie duration provided by the affiliate program. A longer cookie duration means you'll earn commissions for a more extended period after a user clicks on your affiliate link. Look for programs with longer cookie durations to increase your chances of earning commissions. A 30-day referral period is an excellent baseline.

Payment Terms: Consider the payment terms of the affiliate program. Look for programs that offer timely and reliable payments, whether monthly, bi-monthly, or upon reaching a certain earnings threshold. Review the available payment methods to ensure they are convenient for you.

Tracking and Reporting: Evaluate the tracking and reporting capabilities of the affiliate program. Robust tracking and reporting tools provide insights into your performance, allowing you to optimize your efforts and make informed decisions.

Promotional Resources: Determine the availability of promotional resources, such as banners, images, product data feeds, and affiliate support. These resources can help you effectively promote the products or services and enhance your marketing efforts.

Program Reputation and Support: Research the reputation and support provided by the affiliate program. Look for programs with a good track record of paying affiliates on time and offering responsive support if you have any questions or issues.

Program Restrictions and Policies: Review the program's terms and conditions and any restrictions or policies that may affect your promotional activities. Ensure the program's policies align with your marketing strategies and comply with any legal or ethical guidelines you adhere to.

Competitive Landscape: Consider the competition within the affiliate program. Evaluate the number of affiliates already promoting the same products or services and assess the saturation level of the market. Determine if there is room for you to stand out and succeed in promoting the program.

Future Growth Potential: Assess the affiliate program's potential for growth and scalability. Look for programs that continuously add new products or services, expand into new markets, or provide opportunities for recurring commissions.

Where to Find & Join Affiliate Programs

There are several ways to find affiliate programs that align with your niche and interests. Here are some popular methods to discover affiliate programs:

Affiliate Networks: Affiliate networks act as intermediaries between affiliates and merchants, hosting a wide range of affiliate programs. These networks provide a centralized platform to search and apply for multiple affiliate programs.

Directly on Merchant Websites: Many businesses have affiliate programs, which they promote on their websites. If there are specific brands or products, you want to promote, visit their websites and look for an "Affiliate" or "Partner" link in the footer, header, or menu. This link often leads to information about their affiliate program and how to apply.

Affiliate Program Listicles: Many creators publish lists of the best affiliate programs for various niches, for example, the best dating affiliate programs.

Affiliate Program Directories: Online directories compile lists of affiliate programs across various niches and industries. These directories allow you to search for programs based on specific criteria and provide details such as commission rates, cookie durations, and program descriptions.

Industry-specific Websites and Blogs: Explore industry-specific websites and blogs that cater to your niche. They often feature articles or resources related to affiliate marketing and may mention or recommend specific affiliate programs relevant to your niche. Keep an eye out for affiliate program recommendations or affiliate program round-up posts on these platforms.

Social Media Groups and Forums: Engaging with affiliate marketing communities on social media platforms like Facebook, LinkedIn, or Reddit can be a valuable source of information. Join relevant groups or forums where affiliates share insights and recommendations. Members often discuss successful affiliate programs and provide insights into their experiences.

Affiliate Program Aggregators and Sub-Affiliate Networks: Some websites specialize in aggregating affiliate programs across different networks and industries. Examples include FlexOffers and VigLink. These aggregators consolidate multiple programs, making finding and joining various affiliate programs from one platform easier.

Networking and Conferences: Attending industry events, conferences, or networking events can provide direct opportunities to connect with merchants. Many merchants attend such events to promote affiliate programs and build relationships with potential affiliates. Take advantage of networking opportunities to establish connections and learn about new programs.

Recommendations from Peers: Contact fellow affiliates, bloggers, or influencers in your niche and ask for advice. They may have insights into successful affiliate programs or partnerships they have experienced. Building relationships within the affiliate marketing community can lead to valuable recommendations and opportunities.

Image: Freepik.com

Reputable & Established Affiliate Networks

When choosing an affiliate network, consider the range of merchants and products, commission rates, payment terms, reporting tools, and overall reputation. Researching and reading reviews from other affiliates is also beneficial to gain insights into their experiences with different networks. Lastly, before applying to programs, you'll want content on your site, channel, or social media profile. By contrast, no or little content disables the network or merchant from properly assessing your application, usually resulting in rejection.

Several reputable affiliate networks are available, each with its strengths and areas of focus. The best affiliate networks for you will depend on your specific niche, target audience, and marketing goals. Here are some well-regarded affiliate networks that are widely recognized:

Impact is a leading global provider of partnership automation solutions. It offers a user-friendly interface, robust tracking technology, and advanced analytics, enabling businesses and marketers to manage and scale their affiliate programs effectively.

ShareASale is a popular affiliate network known for its wide range of merchants and diverse product categories. It offers a user-friendly interface, robust reporting tools, and reliable payments. ShareASale has a strong reputation in the affiliate marketing industry and is suitable for affiliates across various niches.

CJ Affiliate is one of the largest and most established affiliate networks. It features a vast selection of merchants and offers a comprehensive suite of tracking and reporting tools. CJ Affiliate is mainly known for its strong partnerships with well-known brands and is suitable for affiliates in diverse niches.

FlexOffers offers various affiliate programs across multiple industries and niches, including retail, finance, health, technology, and more. It has a network of thousands of merchants, allowing affiliates to find various products and services to promote to their audience.

Rakuten Advertising is a global affiliate network with many merchants across various industries. It provides a user-friendly platform, comprehensive reporting, and various promotional tools. Rakuten Affiliate Network offers opportunities for affiliates in different niches, including technology, fashion, travel, and more.

Awin is a well-established affiliate network that operates globally. It features a diverse range of merchants and offers competitive commission rates. Awin provides advanced tracking and reporting capabilities and access to various promotional tools. It is suitable for affiliates in multiple niches and industries. ShareASale and Commission Factory join Awin under the Axel Springer and United Internet Groups company umbrella.

<Chapter 7>

COMMISSION PAYMENTS & INCOME

You're munching on a delicious pecan pie on Saturday afternoon. Your phone beeps. It's a sales commission notification for $23.50 from one of your top-performing merchants. You take another bite, sit back, and enjoy the pleasures of making passive income and helping customers make purchases. Experiences like those excite affiliate marketers, and it's why many become publishers in the first place.

Affiliate marketing is an honest way to make good money, and it can be a lucrative venture. It this chapter, we cover various payout models, commissions structures, and secondary income streams.

Cost-Per-Action Models

Several CPA models are commonly used in affiliate marketing, with pay-per-sale and pay-per-lead being the most widespread. Here are some of the most prevalent ones:

Pay-Per-Sale (PPS) or Cost-Per-Sale (CPS): Affiliates earn a commission when a referred visitor purchases on the merchant's website. The commission is usually a percentage of the sale or a fixed amount per sale.

Pay-Per-Lead (PPL) or Cost-Per-Lead (CPL): Affiliates earn a commission for generating qualified leads for the merchant. This typically involves getting visitors to complete a specific action, such as filling out a form, signing up for a trial, or subscribing to a newsletter.

Pay-Per-Click (PPC): Affiliates earn a commission for each click on their affiliate link, regardless of whether a sale or lead is generated. The commission is typically lower than other models and is based solely on driving traffic to the merchant's website.

Pay-Per-Call (PPC): Affiliates earn a commission for each phone call generated through their referral. This model is commonly used in insurance, finance, or consulting industries, where phone inquiries are valuable.

Cost-Per-Install (CPI) or Cost-Per-Download (CPD): Some app developers pay affiliates for each install or download.

Commission Structures

Recurring Commission: Some affiliate programs offer recurring commissions, where affiliates earn a commission for each recurring payment made by a customer they refer. This is common in subscription-based services or membership programs.

Tiered or Performance-Based Commission: In tiered commission structures, affiliates can earn higher commissions as they refer more customers or generate higher sales volumes. For example, they may start with a lower commission rate and progressively increase their commission percentage as they meet certain performance thresholds.

Sub-affiliate Commission: Under the sub-affiliate commission model, affiliates receive additional commissions for recruiting and referring other affiliates to the program. They make a percentage of the referred affiliates' commissions.

Two-Tier Commission: Under the two-tier commission model, affiliates earn commissions for achieving two objectives. For example, an affiliate will earn for getting leads and sales from the leads.

Image: storyset on Freepik.com

Commission Payments

Affiliates receive payments from merchants or affiliate networks based on the agreed-upon terms and payment schedule. The specific payment method available to affiliates depends on the merchant or affiliate network's policies and the affiliate's location.

Affiliates should review the payment methods and schedule the merchant or affiliate network provides before joining an affiliate program. It's also advisable to consider factors such as minimum payment thresholds, payment fees, and any additional requirements for receiving payments.

Affiliates should keep track of their earnings and ensure that they comply with any tax obligations related to their affiliate income. Maintaining accurate records of payments received and associated expenses is essential for financial management and reporting.

Here are the standard methods through which affiliates receive payments:

PayPal is a widely used online payment platform that allows affiliates to accept payments from merchants or affiliate networks. Affiliates must have a PayPal account and provide their email address to receive payments.

Direct Bank Transfer: This method involves the affiliate providing their bank account details to the merchant or affiliate network. Payments are then directly transferred to the affiliate's bank account.

Electronic Funds Transfer (EFT) is a method where payments are directly deposited into the affiliate's bank account, like a direct bank transfer. This method is often used for international payments.

Check: Some merchants or affiliate networks may offer payment by physical checks. Affiliates receive a check in the mail, which they can deposit into their bank account.

Virtual Wallets: Some affiliate networks or platforms offer virtual wallets or payment systems specific to their platform. Affiliates can receive payments into these virtual wallets and may have the option to withdraw the funds to their bank account or use them for other transactions within the platform.

Digital Currencies: Some merchants will pay commissions with cryptos and send funds to the affiliate's crypto address.

Secondary Income Streams

An affiliate's primary source of income will be commissions for sales, leads, and other actions merchants desire. Additionally, affiliates can generate income with the following methods:

Advertising

In the context of content creators, advertising revenue refers to the income generated through advertisements displayed or integrated into their content. Content creators, such as bloggers, YouTubers, podcasters, or website owners, often monetize their platforms by partnering with advertisers or advertising networks to display ads alongside their content.

Advertising revenue is an essential source of income for many content creators. However, the actual revenue earned can vary significantly based on factors such as the size of the audience, the engagement levels, the niche or industry, and the effectiveness of ad placements.

Here's how advertising revenue typically works for content creators:

Ad Placements: Content creators allocate space within their content platforms (e.g., website, YouTube videos, podcasts) for display advertisements. These ads can take various forms, including display ads, video ads, sponsored content, or affiliate links.

Ad Networks or Partnerships: Content creators often collaborate with advertising networks or directly with brands to serve ads on their platforms. Ad networks act as intermediaries, connecting content creators with advertisers and handling the process of ad serving and revenue collection.

Impressions or Clicks: Ad revenue is often generated based on the number of impressions (views) or clicks the ads receive. Content creators are compensated for the number of times the ads are displayed (CPM - cost per thousand impressions) or the number of clicks they generate (CPC - cost per click).

Ad Formats and Pricing: Different ad formats and pricing models exist. For example, display ads may be sold per impression, video ads per view, or sponsored content on a flat fee or performance-based arrangement. The specific terms of the partnership or ad network will determine the pricing structure.

Ad Targeting: Advertisements are often targeted based on factors such as audience demographics, user preferences, and content relevance. Content creators may provide data or insights about their audience to help advertisers deliver more relevant and compelling ads.

Revenue Sharing: Content creators typically receive a portion of the advertising revenue generated from their platforms. The exact revenue share can vary depending on the agreements with ad networks or partnerships.

Ad Performance and Optimization: Content creators may monitor the performance of ads on their platforms, including metrics like click-through rates, conversion rates, or engagement. This data helps optimize ad placements, improve user experience, and maximize revenue potential.

Sponsorship

Sponsorships refer to partnerships between content creators and brands or companies where the brand provides financial support, products, or services in exchange for promotion or endorsement within the content creator's platform. Sponsorships are a form of collaboration that benefits both the content creator and the sponsoring brand.

Content creators should carefully consider sponsorships that align with their values, brand identity, and audience interests to ensure authenticity and maintain trust with their audience. Disclosing sponsorships transparently is essential to maintain ethical practices and comply with applicable regulations or guidelines.

Here are some ways in which content creators can benefit from sponsorships:

Financial Support: Sponsorships can provide content creators with a reliable and often substantial source of income. Brands may offer monetary compensation or cover expenses related to content production, such as equipment, travel, or event attendance.

Expanded Reach and Exposure: Partnering with a brand through sponsorship can help content creators widen their reach and gain exposure to new audiences. Brands often have established customer bases and marketing channels, allowing content creators to tap into these existing networks.

Enhanced Credibility and Authority: Sponsorships can boost content creators' credibility and authority within their niche or industry. When a reputable brand associates itself with a content creator, it adds trust and validation to its content, potentially attracting more followers, subscribers, or readers.

Access to Resources and Opportunities: Sponsoring brands may provide content creators with resources, such as products, software licenses, or professional services, that can enhance the quality and value of their content. They may also offer exclusive opportunities, such as attending industry events, collaborating with other influencers, or gaining early access to new products or services.

Collaborative Content Creation: Sponsors often seek collaborations where content creators create dedicated content featuring their products or services. These collaborations can spark creativity and allow content creators to experiment with new formats, styles, or topics. Collaborative content can also result in engaging and valuable content for the creator's audience.

Long-Term Partnerships: Successful sponsorships can lead to long-term partnerships between content creators and brands. These ongoing relationships can provide a stable and continuous stream of subsidies, offering content creators a consistent revenue source and collaboration opportunities.

Product & Service Sales

Many affiliates double as online retailers, course instructors, authors, freelancers, coaches, consultants, etc. Here are some examples of products and services affiliates sell:

- A social media marketer designs and sells apparel on print-on-demand (POD) websites like Redbubble and Zazzle.
- A YouTuber sells online courses on Skillshare and Udemy.
- A blogger sells books on Amazon through Kindle Direct Publishing (KDP).
- An internet marketer sells coaching packages covering PPC advertising.

Premium Content & Subscriptions

Premium content, in the context of creators, refers to content of higher quality, value, or exclusivity than their regular or free content offerings. It is content that is typically behind a paywall or requires a subscription or one-time payment to access.

Premium content provides additional value, unique experiences, and deeper engagement to a dedicated segment of the creator's audience. It serves as a way for creators to monetize their expertise, time, and resources while rewarding their most loyal supporters. The specific nature of premium content and pricing will vary depending on the creator's niche, audience, and content format.

Premium content examples include the following:

Exclusive Content: Premium content often offers complete access to content unavailable elsewhere or limited to a select group of subscribers or paying customers. It may include unique articles, videos, podcasts, or bonus material beyond the creator's free or public content.

Enhanced Features or Formats: Premium content may provide additional features, formats, or interactive elements that enrich the user experience. For example, it could include interactive quizzes, downloadable resources, high-definition videos, ad-free viewing, or access to a private community or forum.

In-Depth and Expert Insights: Premium content often delves deeper into a topic, offering more detailed analysis, expert insights, or specialized knowledge. It may provide comprehensive guides, tutorials, case studies, or behind-the-scenes content beyond the surface-level information available in free content.

Early Access or Sneak Peeks: Premium content can offer early access to upcoming content or exclusive previews of forthcoming releases. This creates a sense of exclusivity and rewards dedicated subscribers or customers with a first look at new content before it becomes widely available.

Personalized or Customized Content: Some creators offer premium content personalized or customized to the needs or preferences of individual subscribers. This could include personalized coaching, mentoring, tailored advice, or access to one-on-one consultations or Q&A sessions.

Memberships or Subscription Models: Creators may offer premium content through membership or subscription models, where subscribers pay a recurring fee to access benefits and content on an ongoing basis. This provides a consistent revenue stream for creators and ensures continued access to premium offerings for subscribers.

Exclusive Events or Experiences: Premium content can include access to exclusive events, workshops, webinars, or live-streamed sessions with the creator. These events may offer interactive opportunities, direct engagement, or networking with like-minded individuals.

Platform Monetization Tools

YouTube, Facebook, Instagram, and other platforms constantly launch monetization tools to support creators. For example, YouTube offers Super Chats, Super Stickers, Super Thanks, Merch Self, and different ways to make money alongside its partner program, focusing on advertising revenue.

Donations & Crowdfunding

A creator might request donations or crowdfunding for a project on platforms like Kickstarter and Indiegogo. He might also do a fundraiser to grow his brand and profit from other parts of his business. For instance, fundraising videos are a growing trend among YouTubers.

<Chapter 8>

PERFORMANCE METRICS

Successful and profitable affiliate marketers understand and monitor their results monthly to guide their marketing and content activities. Also, they take a holistic view of their operations, not only the bottom line. This brief chapter reviews several critical performance metrics to help grow your affiliate marketing business.

Performance Metrics

Tracking performance is crucial for affiliate marketers to understand the effectiveness of their marketing efforts and optimize their strategies. Affiliate networks and market apps often offer comprehensive dashboards, reporting, and analytics to monitor performance metrics.

Here are some standard metrics or key performance indicators (KPIs) to track your outcomes:

Clicks: Monitor the number of clicks on your affiliate links to gauge your audience's interest and engagement level. This helps you assess the effectiveness of your promotional efforts in driving traffic to the merchant's website.

Conversions: Track the number of conversions or desired actions completed by users who clicked on your affiliate links. This could include sales, sign-ups, downloads, or any other predetermined activities that generate revenue or value for the merchant.

Conversion Rate: Calculate the conversion rate by dividing the number of conversions by the total number of clicks. This metric helps you understand the percentage of visitors who convert after clicking on your affiliate links, indicating your ability to drive desired actions.

Earnings and Revenue: Keep track of your profits and payments generated through affiliate marketing using spreadsheets like Google Docs and Microsoft Excel. Monitor the commissions earned for successful conversions or sales. This helps you assess the profitability of your affiliate programs/campaigns and identify high-performing products or promotions.

Earnings per click (EPC): EPC is a performance metric used in affiliate marketing to measure the average revenue an affiliate earns per click on their affiliate links. It helps affiliates understand the profitability and effectiveness of their marketing efforts in driving conversions.

Return on Investment (ROI): Calculate the ROI by comparing your earnings with the costs incurred in running your affiliate marketing activities. Consider advertising expenses, website hosting fees, digital marketing tools, or other costs associated with promoting affiliate products. Analyzing ROI helps you determine the profitability of your affiliate marketing business.

Other Metrics

Average Order Value (AOV): AOV is used in e-commerce and retail to measure the average value of each customer order. AOV is calculated by dividing the total revenue generated from orders by the total number of orders within a specific period.

Audience Engagement: Assess the engagement levels of your audience through metrics such as comments, shares, likes, or social media interactions. This qualitative data helps gauge the interest and response to your affiliate content, helps with content ideation, and can provide insights into your audience's preferences and behavior.

<Chapter 9>

INTRODUCTION TO CHATGPT

A new product, service, or software takes the world by storm every few years. ChatGPT is the latest to do that, with millions of users globally within a few months. Its capabilities are mind-blowing, and its potential is limitless. Many people and groups have noticed, including governments, business leaders, and entertainers. On the other hand, ChatGPT is just one more AI innovation. Specifically, machine learning is a field of AI that allows systems to learn and improve from experience without being explicitly programmed. ChatGPT is one of those systems, and we explore it in this chapter by discussing what it is, how it works, pros, cons, and alternatives.

What Is ChatGPT?

ChatGPT is a language model developed by OpenAI. It belongs to the GPT (Generative Pre-trained Transformer) family of models. GPT models are designed to generate human-like text responses given a prompt or a series of input text. The "Chat" in ChatGPT signifies that it is optimized explicitly for conversational interactions.

ChatGPT is trained on a vast amount of diverse text data from the internet, allowing it to learn patterns, grammar, and context in language. It can understand and generate text conversationally, making it suitable for various applications such as chatbots, virtual assistants, and other dialogue systems.

The model is built upon a Transformer architecture, a deep learning model that utilizes self-attention mechanisms to capture relationships between words in a sentence. This architecture allows ChatGPT to understand and generate coherent and contextually relevant responses effectively.

ChatGPT does not possess proper understanding or consciousness as an AI language model. It generates responses based on patterns learned from data, and while it can provide helpful and relevant information, its responses should be carefully evaluated for accuracy and reliability.

The cost of using ChatGPT or any other AI service can vary depending on the version, usage, service level, and the platform or provider you choose. For example, it costs $20 monthly to access the premium or latest version of ChatGPT.

How ChatGPT Works

Users can interact with ChatGPT by conversing through a user interface or an application that integrates the model. Here's a general outline of how users can use ChatGPT:

- Access the interface: Users typically access ChatGPT through a user interface, such as a chat window on a website, a messaging app, or a voice-based interface. The interface allows users to input their queries or prompts and receive responses from ChatGPT.
- Provide a prompt: Users enter their query or prompt in natural language. It can be a question, a statement, or any text conveying their intent or the information they seek. For example, "What is the capital of France?" or "Can you help me troubleshoot my computer issue?"
- Receive a response: Once the prompt is submitted, ChatGPT processes the input and generates a response based on its training and learned patterns. The answer is then displayed in the user interface or conveyed through the chosen medium, such as text, voice, or both.
- Continue the conversation: Users can continue by providing follow-up questions or additional context based on the generated response. This allows for an interactive and iterative exchange with ChatGPT.
- Iterate and refine: If the initial response doesn't fully address the user's query or further clarification is

needed, the user can refine their prompt or provide more details to guide ChatGPT toward a more accurate response.

- Evaluate and act: Users evaluate the generated responses and act accordingly. They can consider the information provided, ask for further clarification, seek additional sources, or act based on the insights gained from the conversation.

To make the most efficient use of ChatGPT, consider the following tips:

- Be clear and specific: Provide a clear and particular prompt to help guide ChatGPT's response. Clearly state what information or assistance you are seeking. For example, instead of asking, "Tell me about dogs," you can ask, "What are the most common breeds of dogs?"
- Use system messages: You can use system-level instructions to guide ChatGPT's behavior. For instance, you can specify the desired format of the answer or ask it to think step-by-step before responding. System messages help set expectations for the model and can improve the quality of the generated responses.
- Experiment with temperature and max tokens: Temperature and max tokens can be adjusted during inference. Temperature controls the randomness of the output, with lower values making the responses more focused and deterministic, while higher values introduce more randomness. Max tokens limit the length of the generated response. Adjusting these parameters can help you tailor the response length and level of creativity to your preference.
- Iterate and clarify: If the initial response from ChatGPT is unsatisfactory or doesn't fully address your query, you can iterate by providing additional context or asking follow-up questions. This can help guide the model toward generating more accurate and relevant responses.

- Critical evaluation: While ChatGPT is designed to provide helpful information, it's essential to evaluate its responses critically. Double-check the accuracy and reliability of the information provided, especially for sensitive or important topics. ChatGPT does not have real-time access to updated information, so verify its responses with trusted sources when necessary.
- Report issues and give feedback: If you encounter incorrect or concerning responses from ChatGPT, provide input to OpenAI or the organization implementing the model. Reporting issues helps improve the model and ensures ongoing refinements for better performance and safety.
- Remember that ChatGPT is a language model and not a human expert. While it can provide valuable information, it's essential to verify its responses and not solely rely on them for critical decisions or sensitive matters.

Image: storyset on Freepik.com

Mastering Prompts

To improve your prompts and get better results from ChatGPT, you can consider the following tips:

Make your prompt more explicit: Instead of asking open-ended or ambiguous questions, try to be more specific and provide clear instructions or guidelines. The more detailed your prompt is, the easier it will be for the model to understand your expectations.

Add relevant context: Providing additional context or background information about the topic can help the model generate more accurate and appropriate responses. Include relevant details, facts, or any requirements that might be important for the prompt.

Specify the desired output format: If you have a particular structure in mind for the response (e.g., bullet points, step-by-step instructions, pros and cons), mention it explicitly in your prompt. This can guide the model's response and provide the desired output structure.

Experiment with different phrasings: If the initial response doesn't meet your expectations, try rephrasing or restructuring your prompt. Sometimes, small changes in wording or structure can lead to significantly different and more relevant responses.

Use examples or templates: Including examples or templates in your prompt can give the model a clear idea of the desired response format. You can provide a sample answer or specify the key points you expect the response to cover.

Ask the model to think step-by-step: If you want it to provide a more detailed or logical reasoning process, you can explicitly ask it to think step-by-step or explain its thought process. This can result in more comprehensive and insightful responses.

Provide feedback: If the model's initial response doesn't meet your expectations, you can provide feedback and iterate on the conversation. Engaging in a back-and-forth dialogue with the model can help you guide it toward generating more accurate and helpful responses.

Leverage the model's strengths: ChatGPT performs well in generating text-based content, offering explanations, creative writing, and general knowledge. You can leverage these strengths by focusing your prompts on these areas.

Balance specificity and creativity: While being specific in your prompts is essential, remember that the model can sometimes generate creative and unexpected responses. Find a balance between guiding the model and allowing it to provide unique insights or perspectives.

Explore the capabilities of ChatGPT: Experiment with different types of prompts to explore the model's capabilities. You can ask it to summarize an article, debate pros, and cons, brainstorm ideas, or even engage in creative storytelling.

ChatGPT Pros & Cons

ChatGPT, like any AI language model, has pros and cons. Here are some of them.

Pros

Access to vast knowledge: ChatGPT has been trained on a wide range of internet text, giving it access to enormous amounts of information. It can provide answers, explanations, and insights on various topics.

Language generation capabilities: ChatGPT can generate coherent and contextually relevant responses, making it helpful in drafting emails, developing ideas, or even creative writing.

Availability and convenience: ChatGPT can be accessed anytime and anywhere with an internet connection. It provides a convenient way to obtain information, get assistance, or engage in conversations.

Learning and exploration: Interacting with ChatGPT can be a valuable learning experience. It can introduce new concepts and perspectives and even help you explore creative ideas.

Assistance and productivity: ChatGPT can assist with tasks such as summarizing articles, providing suggestions, or helping with problem-solving. It can be a valuable tool for boosting productivity and efficiency.

Cons

Potential inaccuracies and biases: ChatGPT generates responses based on patterns it has learned from the training data, which can lead to inaccuracies or biased outputs. It may only sometimes provide correct or reliable information, so fact-checking is essential.

Lack of critical thinking: ChatGPT doesn't possess real-world understanding or critical thinking abilities. It can provide answers based on patterns it has learned, but it may only sometimes comprehend a question's context or underlying meaning.

Ethical concerns: Ethical considerations surround the use of AI language models like ChatGPT. Privacy, security, and responsible use of AI must be addressed to prevent misuse or harmful consequences.

Limited domain knowledge: While ChatGPT can access extensive information, it may need deep expertise in specific domains. Therefore, it may only sometimes provide specialized or highly technical insights.

Dependency and overreliance: Relying solely on ChatGPT for information and decision-making can be risky. Recognizing its limitations and supplement its responses with information from credible sources or expert advice is essential.

Lack of personal touch: ChatGPT is an AI language model, and it doesn't have human emotions or empathy. It may not fully understand or respond to emotional or personal queries like a human would.

It's crucial to be aware of these pros and cons while using ChatGPT and to exercise critical thinking and caution when interpreting its responses. Using it as a tool in conjunction with human judgment and multiple sources of information can help mitigate some of the limitations and enhance its benefits.

ChatGPT Alternatives

While ChatGPT is a popular AI language model, there are several alternatives available that you can explore. Here are some notable ones:

Bard by Google is an extensive language model from Google AI, trained on a massive dataset of text and code. It can generate text, translate languages, write creative content, and answer questions.

HuggingChat is a chatbot framework that uses Hugging Face's transformers library. It is easy to use and can be customized to suit your needs.

Bing AI is a conversational search engine that uses GPT-4 to power conversations. It can answer questions in a comprehensive and informative way.

Sparrow by DeepMind is a chatbot still under development, but it can be one of the best ChatGPT alternatives. It can learn and adapt to its users, and it can generate text that is both informative and engaging.

YouChat is an AI search assistant allowing users to have human-like conversations in their search results. It is powered by GPT-3 and can answer questions, generate text, and even translate languages.

Chatsonic is a chatbot that is designed explicitly for factual content creation. It can generate text, translate languages, and write creative content.

Perplexity AI is a conversational search engine that enables users to get answers to questions on any number of topics. It is powered by GPT-3 and can access and process information from the real world through Google Search.

<Chapter 10>

CHATGPT FOR AFFILIATES & CREATORS

Affiliate marketing in isolation isn't how affiliates make money. Instead, affiliates require at least one profile and platform to distribute affiliate links and earn commissions. For example, an affiliate blogs (a blogger) and uses her WordPress website (the platform) to promote pet products. Therefore, we must review how ChatGPT can support various affiliate profiles, which we'll do in this chapter.

ChatGPT for Bloggers

ChatGPT can support bloggers in several activities:

Idea Generation: Bloggers often need a constant stream of new ideas to keep their content fresh and engaging. ChatGPT can generate creative prompts or brainstorming suggestions for blog post topics, helping bloggers explore new angles, trends, or unique perspectives to captivate their audience.

Content Generation: Bloggers must produce high-quality content to engage their audience consistently. ChatGPT can assist by generating blog post ideas, suggesting subtopics, providing introductions or outlines, or even writing portions of the content. This can help bloggers overcome writer's block, save time, and generate fresh and unique content.

Research Assistance: ChatGPT can help bloggers research by providing relevant information, statistics, or references on specific topics. It can gather data, provide insights, or summarize complex concepts, enabling bloggers to create well-informed and authoritative content.

Content Editing and Proofreading: Bloggers can use ChatGPT to review and edit their content for clarity, grammar, and readability. It can help identify spelling or punctuation errors, suggest alternative wordings, or provide language improvements to enhance the overall quality of the blog posts.

SEO Optimization: ChatGPT can guide you in optimizing blog posts for search engines. It can suggest relevant keywords, meta tags, or headers that can improve the blog's search engine visibility and ranking. By incorporating SEO best practices, bloggers can attract more organic traffic.

Language Translation: For bloggers who target an international audience, ChatGPT can assist with language translation. It can provide translations of blog posts or help generate content in multiple languages, expanding the reach and readership of the blog.

ChatGPT prompt examples for bloggers include the following:

- "Generate a list of 10 blog post ideas related to [chosen niche]."
- "Help me outline a blog post on the topic of [specific keyword]."
- "Suggest ways to optimize my blog for better SEO and organic traffic."
- "Assist me in creating an engaging introduction for my latest blog post."
- "Generate a conclusion paragraph for my article about [chosen topic]."

ChatGPT for YouTubers

ChatGPT can be a helpful tool for YouTube creators in the following ways:

Content Ideas: ChatGPT can assist YouTube creators by generating video content ideas based on specific topics, keywords, or niches. It can provide creative prompts or suggest unique angles to help creators develop engaging and appealing video concepts.

Scriptwriting Assistance: Writing a compelling script is crucial for creating engaging YouTube videos. ChatGPT can help YouTube creators by providing suggestions, outlines, or drafting script sections. It can assist in structuring the content, improving storytelling, and enhancing the overall flow of the video.

Audience Engagement: ChatGPT can help YouTube creators engage with their audience by generating responses to comments, questions, or interactions on their YouTube channel. It can provide personalized and engaging replies, fostering a sense of connection and community with viewers.

Video Editing Tips: ChatGPT can offer insights and suggestions for editing techniques, transitions, or visual effects that can enhance the overall quality of the videos. It can recommend editing software, video filters, or music choices to help create visually appealing and professional-looking content.

SEO Optimization: YouTube creators need to optimize their video titles, descriptions, tags, and thumbnails for better visibility in search results. ChatGPT can guide keyword research, suggest relevant tags, or help craft compelling titles and descriptions that improve search engine rankings and attract more viewers.

Collaborations and Guest Ideas: ChatGPT can assist YouTube creators in identifying potential collaborators or guests for their videos. By providing information about the creator's niche or target audience, ChatGPT can suggest relevant channels or personalities that align with their content and foster valuable collaborations.

Trend Analysis: Staying current with the latest trends is essential for YouTube creators. ChatGPT can help identify emerging trends, popular topics, or viral content within the creator's niche. This information can guide creators in creating timely, relevant videos that capture the audience's attention.

ChatGPT prompt examples for YouTubers include the following:

- "Provide me with a script outline for a YouTube video on [specific topic]."

- "Suggest editing techniques to make my YouTube videos more engaging."
- "Help me develop a catchy title for my next YouTube video."
- "Generate a list of video tags to optimize the SEO of my YouTube channel."
- "Assist me in creating an engaging thumbnail for my latest YouTube video."

ChatGPT for Podcasters

ChatGPT can help podcasters in many of the same ways it can help YouTubers, including content generation, scriptwriting and outlining, interview prep, editing, and audience engagement. Additionally, ChatGPT can assist podcasters in creating show notes or episode descriptions. It can summarize the episode's main points, highlight key takeaways, or provide links to relevant resources mentioned in the episode. ChatGPT can assist in crafting compelling and informative descriptions that attract potential listeners and improve discoverability.

Consider the following ChatGPT prompt ideas for podcasters:

- "Generate a list of potential interview questions for my upcoming podcast episode."
- "Help me outline the structure and segments for my next podcast episode."
- "Assist me in writing the show notes for my latest podcast episode."
- "Suggest strategies to increase engagement and listener interaction on my podcast."
- "Provide recommendations for promoting my podcast on social media platforms."

ChatGPT for Social Media Marketers & Influencers

ChatGPT can provide valuable assistance to social media marketers and influencers in these ways:

Content Creation: ChatGPT can help generate creative and engaging ideas for social media posts, captions, or video scripts. It can provide inspiration, suggest trending topics, or offer unique angles to keep the content fresh and appealing to the target audience.

Audience Engagement: ChatGPT can assist social media marketers, and influencers in engaging with their audience by generating personalized responses to comments, messages, or mentions. It can help maintain an active and interactive presence, fostering a sense of connection and building stronger relationships with followers.

Trend Analysis: Keeping up with the latest trends and viral content is essential in social media marketing. ChatGPT can help identify emerging trends, popular hashtags, or viral topics within specific niches or industries. It can provide insights and suggestions for creating content that aligns with current trends, increasing the chances of gaining visibility and engagement.

Influencer Campaigns: ChatGPT can assist social media marketers in planning and executing influencer marketing campaigns. It can help identify suitable influencers based on target demographics, engagement rates, or content relevance. ChatGPT can also generate collaboration ideas or suggest creative ways to leverage influencer partnerships for maximum impact.

Social Media Advertising: ChatGPT can provide insights and recommendations for advertising campaigns. It can assist in defining target audiences, optimizing ad content, or identifying the most effective ad formats and placements. This can help social media marketers and influencers achieve better reach, engagement, and conversion rates through paid advertising.

Analytics and Performance Tracking: ChatGPT can help social media marketers and influencers analyze social media metrics such as follower growth, engagement rates, or click-through rates. It can provide insights and suggestions based on the data, allowing for data-driven decision-making and continuous improvement of social media strategies.

Brand Partnerships: ChatGPT can assist influencers in identifying potential brand partnerships or sponsorships. ChatGPT can suggest relevant brands or collaboration opportunities that align with the influencer's values and content style by providing information about the influencer's niche, target audience, or brand preferences.

ChatGPT prompt examples for social media marketers include the following:

- "Suggest content ideas for an engaging social media post related to [chosen topic]."
- "Help me craft a compelling headline and caption for my latest social media post."
- "Assist me in optimizing my social media profiles for better brand visibility."
- "Generate ideas for a social media campaign to promote a new product/service."
- "Provide insights on the best times to post on different social media platforms."

ChatGPT for Email Marketers

ChatGPT can provide assistance to email marketers in these areas:

Segmentation and Targeting: ChatGPT can assist email marketers in segmenting their email lists and targeting specific audience segments. By providing information about customer demographics, preferences, or behaviors, ChatGPT can suggest segmentation strategies and help personalize email content to cater to the interests and needs of different customer groups.

Automation and Drip Campaigns: ChatGPT can help email marketers set up and optimize automated email sequences or drip campaigns. It can suggest the ideal timing, frequency, and content flow for different stages of the customer journey, ensuring subscribers receive relevant and timely emails to nurture engagement and conversion.

A/B Testing: Testing and optimizing email campaigns is crucial for improving performance. ChatGPT can provide insights and recommendations for A/B testing variations of email subject lines, content, or call-to-action buttons. It can suggest testing hypotheses, analyze results, and provide guidance on optimizing email elements based on data-driven insights.

Personalization and Dynamic Content: ChatGPT can assist email marketers in personalizing email content based on individual subscriber data. It can generate dynamic content elements, such as personalized product recommendations, tailored offers, or customized greetings. ChatGPT can help create a personalized and relevant email experience that resonates with recipients and increases engagement.

Email Analytics and Reporting: ChatGPT can help email marketers analyze email campaign performance metrics, such as open rates, click-through rates, or conversion rates. It can generate insights and suggestions based on the data, assisting in identifying trends, optimizing email strategies, and improving future email campaigns.

Compliance and Best Practices: ChatGPT can guide email marketing best practices and compliance with relevant regulations, such as GDPR or CAN-SPAM. It can suggest strategies for building a permission-based email list, implementing unsubscribe mechanisms, or ensuring data privacy and security.

Content Generation: Writing engaging and persuasive email content is essential for marketing campaigns. ChatGPT can help email marketers generate ideas, subject lines, or even email drafts. It can provide suggestions for personalization, storytelling, or crafting compelling calls-to-action, helping to increase open rates, click-through rates, and conversions.

ChatGPT prompt examples for email marketers include the following:

- "Help me create an engaging subject line for my next email marketing campaign."
- "Suggest ways to improve my email newsletters' open and click-through rates."
- "Assist me in crafting a personalized email sequence for a new subscriber onboarding."
- "Generate content ideas for a promotional email about a new product/service."
- "Provide tips on segmenting my email list for targeted and effective email campaigns."

ChatGPT for Internet & PPC Marketers

ChatGPT can assist performance marketers in the following ways:

Ad Copy Generation: ChatGPT can help performance marketers generate compelling ad copy for various advertising platforms, including search ads, social media ads, display ads, and more. It can assist in crafting attention-grabbing headlines, persuasive body text, and compelling calls to action to maximize click-through rates and conversions.

Landing Page Optimization: ChatGPT can assist performance marketers in optimizing their landing pages for better conversion rates. It can provide suggestions for improving the layout, content, and design of landing pages to enhance user experience and encourage desired actions. ChatGPT can generate landing page variations for A/B testing to identify the most compelling versions.

Targeting and Segmentation Strategies: ChatGPT can provide insights and suggestions on targeting and segmentation strategies for performance marketing campaigns. It can assist in identifying relevant audience segments, refining targeting criteria, and optimizing campaign parameters to reach the right audience with personalized messages and offers.

Keyword Research: ChatGPT can assist performance marketers in keyword research and optimization for search engine marketing (SEM) campaigns. It can suggest relevant keywords, long-tail variations, and negative keywords to refine targeting and improve ad relevance. ChatGPT can also generate keyword-rich ad copy to enhance the quality of the ad and its performance.

Performance Analysis: ChatGPT can help performance marketers analyze campaign performance data and generate insights. It can assist in identifying trends, patterns, and opportunities for optimization. ChatGPT can also provide recommendations for adjusting bidding strategies, targeting parameters, or creative elements to improve campaign performance and ROI.

Competitive Analysis: ChatGPT can help performance marketers conduct a competitive analysis to gain insights into competitors' strategies and identify opportunities for differentiation. It can assist in analyzing competitor ad copy, landing pages, keyword targeting, and positioning. ChatGPT can provide suggestions for improving campaign messaging, unique selling propositions, or value propositions based on the competitive landscape.

Budget Allocation and Optimization: ChatGPT can recommend budget allocation and optimization for performance marketing campaigns. It can assist in determining the most effective distribution of advertising spend across channels, campaigns, or ad variations. ChatGPT can also suggest bid adjustments, budget reallocation, or pacing strategies to maximize campaign performance within budget constraints.

ChatGPT prompts for internet marketers include the following examples:

- "Help me optimize my Google Ads campaign for better conversion rates."
- "Suggest strategies to improve my Facebook ad's landing page conversion rate."

- "Assist me in analyzing and interpreting my PPC campaign performance data."
- "Generate ad copy variations for split testing in my display advertising campaign."
- "Provide insights on audience targeting and segmentation for my performance marketing campaigns."

ChatGPT for Course Creators

ChatGPT can be a valuable resource for course creators in these ways:

Content Development: ChatGPT can assist course creators in developing course content. It can generate ideas for lessons, provide outlines or structures for course modules, and even help with writing sections of the course materials. This can save time and offer fresh perspectives to create engaging and informative course content.

Lesson Planning: ChatGPT can help course creators with lesson planning by suggesting learning objectives, activities, or assessments. It can assist in creating a logical flow of topics and ensure that the course material is organized coherently and effectively.

Instructional Design: ChatGPT can guide instructional design principles. It can help course creators incorporate multimedia elements, interactive activities, or assessments to enhance the learning experience. ChatGPT can suggest strategies to promote learner engagement, knowledge retention, and application of concepts.

Learner Support: ChatGPT can assist course creators in developing resources or tools to support learners. It can generate FAQs, study guides, or additional reference materials to supplement the course content. ChatGPT can also provide personalized responses to learner queries or offer suggestions for creating discussion forums or support communities.

Course Marketing: ChatGPT can assist course creators in marketing their courses. It can help generate compelling course descriptions, suggest keywords for search engine optimization, or provide insights on effective marketing strategies. ChatGPT can also assist in creating promotional materials, such as social media posts or email campaigns, to attract potential learners.

Assessment and Feedback: ChatGPT can assist with creating assessments and feedback mechanisms. It can suggest different types of assessments, such as quizzes or assignments, and help course creators develop clear and concise feedback guidelines to provide valuable input to learners.

Personalization and Adaptation: ChatGPT can help course creators personalize the learning experience for individual learners. It can generate suggestions for adaptive learning pathways based on learner progress or provide tailored recommendations for additional resources or activities to meet learners' needs.

ChatGPT prompt examples for course creators include the following:

- "Help me outline the modules and lessons for my online course on [chosen topic]."
- "Suggest ways to create engaging video lectures for my online course."
- "Assist me in developing an effective course pricing and discount strategy."
- "Generate ideas for bonus content or resources to include in my course."
- "Provide recommendations on marketing and promoting my online course to a target audience."

ChatGPT for eBook Authors

ChatGPT can support ebook authors in the following activities:

Idea Generation: ChatGPT can help ebook authors generate ideas for their books. It can provide suggestions based on different genres, topics, or themes, assisting authors to explore new angles or uncover unique perspectives to make their ebooks stand out.

Outline and Structure: ChatGPT can assist ebook authors in creating a well-organized outline and structure for their book. It can help define chapters, subtopics, or sections, ensuring a logical flow of information and a cohesive reading experience for the audience.

Content Development: ChatGPT can assist ebook authors in developing the content of their books. It can help generate paragraphs, sections, or even complete passages based on the author's input. This can save time and provide fresh perspectives, enhancing the overall quality and depth of the ebook.

Editing and Proofreading: ChatGPT can help ebook authors edit and proofread. It can provide suggestions for improving grammar, syntax, or sentence structure. ChatGPT can also help identify inconsistencies, redundancies, or areas where additional clarification or examples may be needed.

Formatting and Design: ChatGPT can guide ebook formatting and design elements. It can suggest appropriate fonts, layouts, or illustrations to enhance the visual appeal of the ebook. ChatGPT can also assist in optimizing the ebook for different reading devices or platforms.

ChatGPT prompt ideas for ebook authors include the following:

- "Help me create a compelling book title for my upcoming eBook [chosen topic]."
- "Assist me in outlining the chapters and sections for my eBook."
- "Suggest effective strategies for self-publishing and promoting my eBook."
- "Generate ideas for a captivating book cover design for my eBook."
- "Provide tips on formatting and structuring my eBook for a seamless reading experience."

ChatGPT for Website Owners

Alongside content ideas and SEO, ChatGPT can provide excellent support to website owners in several ways:

User Experience (UX) Improvement: ChatGPT can help website owners enhance the user experience of their website. It can suggest website layout, navigation, or overall design improvements. ChatGPT can also provide recommendations for creating intuitive user interfaces, optimizing page load times, or improving mobile responsiveness.

Conversion Rate Optimization (CRO): ChatGPT can assist website owners in optimizing their websites for conversions. It can provide insights on compelling call-to-action (CTA) placement, persuasive copywriting, or landing page optimization. ChatGPT can suggest strategies for improving conversion rates and increasing the likelihood of visitors taking desired actions.

Content Curation: ChatGPT can help website owners curate content from various sources to provide valuable information to their audience. It can assist in summarizing or paraphrasing articles, news pieces, or research findings, ensuring the content is appropriately attributed and relevant to the website's niche or industry.

Customer Support: ChatGPT can assist website owners in providing customer support and answering frequently asked questions. It can help generate responses to common inquiries, provide troubleshooting tips, or direct visitors to relevant resources. ChatGPT can enhance the website's responsiveness and improve the overall customer experience.

Data Analysis and Insights: ChatGPT can help website owners analyze data and generate insights. It can assist in identifying trends, user behavior patterns, or areas of improvement based on analytics reports. ChatGPT can also recommend optimizing website performance, reducing bounce rates, or increasing engagement metrics.

Consider the following ChatGPT prompt examples for website owners:

- "Suggest ways to improve the user experience and navigation of my website."
- "Help me optimize my website for better search engine rankings and organic traffic."
- "Assist me in developing a content strategy to attract and engage visitors on my website."
- "Generate ideas for lead generation tactics to grow my email subscriber list."
- "Provide recommendations for website monetization strategies and revenue streams."

Other Excellent AI Tools

This chapter and book focus on ChatGPT as a helpful tool for affiliate marketers of all stripes. However, your journey shouldn't stop there. Instead, various AI tools exist for each affiliate profile, platform, content creator, and marketer to support your goals. Here's a short list of other tools to review.

Grammarly is a grammar checker that uses AI to help you improve your writing. It can identify grammar errors, spelling mistakes, and punctuation errors.

Hemingway Editor is a writing editor that uses AI to help you make your writing clearer and more concise. It highlights areas of your writing that are difficult to read and suggests ways to improve your writing.

Jasper.ai is an AI writing assistant that can help you create high-quality content quickly and easily. It can generate blog posts, marketing copy, and social media posts.

Copy.ai is another AI writing assistant to help you with your content creation needs. It can generate ad copy, email subject lines, product descriptions, and more.

Rytr is an AI writing tool that can help you with your blog posts, social media posts, and other content. It can also help you with your grammar and punctuation.

Closerscopy is an AI copywriting tool that can help you create high-converting sales copy. It can generate email subject lines, landing pages, and more.

Outgrow is an AI-powered content creation platform that can help you create interactive content, such as quizzes, calculators, and surveys.

MarketMuse is an AI-powered content optimization tool that can help you improve your website's SEO. It analyzes your content and improves keyword usage, readability, and overall SEO score.

Semrush is another SEO tool that uses AI to help you improve your website's SEO. Its features include keyword research, backlink analysis, and on-page SEO optimization.

BuzzSumo is a social media analytics tool that uses AI to help you track the performance of your social media content. It can also help you find relevant influencers to promote your content.

Later is a social media scheduling tool that uses AI to help you create and schedule your social media posts. It can also help you track the performance of your posts and optimize your social media strategy.

Buffer is another social media scheduling tool that uses AI to help you create and schedule your social media posts. It also has various other features, such as analytics and collaboration tools.

TubeBuddy is a YouTube management tool that uses AI to help you optimize your videos for search. It can help you find keywords, track your analytics, and improve your video titles and descriptions.

VidIQ is another YouTube management tool that uses AI to help you improve your channel's performance. It can help you find the right keywords, track your analytics, and create engaging thumbnails.

Thumbnail Maker is an AI-powered tool that can help you create eye-catching thumbnails for your YouTube videos. It uses AI to analyze your videos and create thumbnails likely to attract viewers.

InVideo is an AI-powered video editing tool that can help you create professional-looking videos without editing experience. It has a library of templates, effects, and music that you can use, and it also has an AI assistant that can help you with your editing decisions.

Synthesia is an AI-powered video editing tool to help you create narrated videos with hyper-realistic AI avatars. It uses AI to generate text-to-speech and lip-syncing, so you can create videos without appearing on camera.

Lumen5 is an AI-powered video editing tool that can help you create engaging videos quickly and easily. It has a library of templates, music, and effects that you can use, and it also has an AI assistant that can help you with your editing decisions.

StreamYard is an AI-powered live streaming platform that can help you create professional-looking live streams. It can automatically generate captions, track analytics, and more.

Be.Live Comment Assistant is an AI-powered tool to help moderate your live streams. It can automatically detect and remove spam comments and suggest relevant comments for you to reply to.

Descript's AI-powered video editing tool can help you transcribe your videos, edit the transcripts, and generate new videos from the transcripts. It uses AI to analyze your videos and create transcripts that are accurate and easy to read.

<Chapter 11>

CONCLUSION & START YOUR JOURNEY

This book has comprehensively explored the powerful synergy between affiliate marketing and ChatGPT. We have delved into the fundamental concepts of affiliate marketing, examined the role of ChatGPT in enhancing marketing strategies, and explored the various ways content creators can leverage this AI technology to optimize their affiliate campaigns. Throughout this journey, we have discovered how ChatGPT can revolutionize the affiliate marketing landscape by providing valuable insights, content generation support, and automation capabilities.

Content creators can tap into many opportunities by integrating ChatGPT into their affiliate marketing efforts. They can benefit from AI-powered content generation, enabling them to produce high-quality, engaging content at scale. Additionally, ChatGPT can assist in audience targeting, keyword research, and campaign optimization, helping marketers achieve better conversion rates and higher revenue. With ChatGPT's ability to analyze data, generate insights, and provide personalized recommendations, content creators can make data-driven decisions and adapt their strategies for optimal results.

Next Steps

As you conclude this book, it is essential to remember that affiliate marketing and AI technology constantly evolve. To stay ahead and maximize your success, consider the following next steps:

Stay Updated: Stay informed about the latest trends and advancements in affiliate marketing and AI technologies like

ChatGPT. Follow industry experts, attend webinars or conferences, and engage in online communities to remain up-to-date.

Test and Experiment: Implement the strategies and techniques discussed in this book but be bold and experiment. Test different approaches, monitor performance, and adapt accordingly. Embrace a mindset of continuous improvement and optimization.

Cultivate Relationships: Build strong relationships with affiliate networks, merchants, and fellow marketers. Collaborate, share insights, and leverage each other's experiences. Networking and partnerships can open doors to new opportunities and expand your reach.

Monitor Analytics: Regularly track and analyze your affiliate marketing performance metrics. Leverage tools like Google Analytics and affiliate network reporting to gain insights into what's working and what can be improved. Make data-driven decisions to refine your strategies.

Embrace Innovation: Stay open to new technologies and innovations that can enhance your affiliate marketing efforts. As AI evolves, explore new tools and platforms that can augment your capabilities and provide a competitive edge.

Remember, success in affiliate marketing requires persistence, adaptability, and a commitment to continuous learning. Alternatively, taking shortcuts and seeking get-rich schemes will lead to disappointing outcomes and potential legal problems. By harnessing the power of ChatGPT and leveraging the strategies outlined in this book, you are well on your way to becoming a proficient and successful affiliate marketer in the digital age. Best of luck on your journey!

<Chapter 12>

FREQUENTLY ASKED QUESTIONS

Although we covered various affiliate marketing topics, let's review common questions from aspiring affiliates.

What should be my primary goals as an affiliate marketer?

Your primary goal should revolve around driving consistent and sustainable revenue while providing value to your audience. Here are some other key goals to focus on:

Generate Sales and Conversions: Your goal is to drive sales and conversions for the affiliate products or services you promote. Aim to increase the number of purchases made through your affiliate links and track your conversion rates to gauge your effectiveness.

Build Trust and Credibility: Prioritize building trust and credibility with your audience. You establish yourself as an authority in your niche by consistently delivering valuable and relevant content. This trust will increase the likelihood of your audience following your recommendations and purchasing through your affiliate links.

Grow Your Audience: Work towards expanding your audience and attracting targeted traffic to your website, blog, or social media platforms. Focus on increasing the number of engaged and loyal followers interested in your niche and more likely to convert into customers.

Provide Value to Your Audience: Always prioritize providing value through informative and engaging content. Your goal should be to address their needs, solve their problems, and offer helpful recommendations that align with their interests and preferences. You build a loyal audience base that trusts your proposals by delivering value.

Optimize Conversion Rates: Continually improve your conversion rates by optimizing various aspects of your affiliate marketing strategy. This includes optimizing your landing pages, call-to-action buttons, content structure, and persuasive techniques. Experiment with different approaches, test, and analyze the results to refine your strategies.

Diversify Revenue Streams: While affiliate marketing is your primary focus, consider diversifying your revenue streams. Explore additional monetization methods such as sponsored content, display advertising, or creating and selling your products or courses. Diversification can provide stability and increase your income potential.

How much does it cost to join affiliate networks and programs as a publisher?

It costs nothing to join affiliate networks and programs. Instead, affiliate networks earn revenue from charging merchants' fees, such as software subscription fees and commission overrides. Merchants benefit from marketers promoting their goods and paying only for sales and other actions.

How many affiliate programs should I join?

The number of affiliate programs you should join as an affiliate marketer depends on various factors, including your niche, audience, marketing strategy, and available time and resources. While there is no specific limit, balancing quality and quantity is essential. Here are some considerations to help you determine the correct number of affiliate programs to join:

Relevance to Your Niche: Focus on affiliate programs that align with your niche and your audience's interests. Promoting products or services that are relevant and valuable to your audience is better than joining numerous programs with unrelated offerings.

Quality and Reputation: Prioritize joining reputable and established affiliate programs that offer high-quality products or services. Look for programs with reliable tracking, timely payments, and reasonable commission rates. Working with a few reliable programs is generally more beneficial than joining numerous low-quality ones.

Diversification: While focusing on a few critical programs is essential, diversifying your income sources can be beneficial. Consider joining programs that offer a variety of products or services within your niche, allowing you to cater to different segments of your audience and mitigate risks associated with relying on a single program.

Time and Resources: Assess the amount of time and resources you can dedicate to managing multiple affiliate programs effectively. Each program requires attention, including monitoring performance, creating content, and optimizing campaigns. Ensure you can commit time and effort to deliver quality promotion for each program you join.

Commission Potential: Evaluate the commission rates and earning potential of the affiliate programs you consider. Some programs may offer higher or recurring commissions, impacting your overall revenue. Balance your selection based on the potential return on investment for your efforts.

Performance Tracking: It's crucial to effectively track each affiliate program's performance to assess its profitability. Ensure you have the necessary tracking tools and systems to monitor and analyze the results of each program.

Ultimately, the ideal number of affiliate programs to join will vary for each affiliate marketer. Start with a manageable number that allows you to effectively promote and manage the programs and gradually expand as you gain experience and succeed. When selecting affiliate programs, quality, relevance, and alignment with your audience's needs should be the primary considerations.

What should I do if an affiliate network or merchant declines my application?

It can be unpleasant if an affiliate network or merchant declines your application. However, rejection is a standard part of the affiliate marketing experience. Use it as an opportunity to learn, grow, and refine your approach. With persistence, continuous improvement, and a strong focus on providing value to your audience, you can increase your chances of acceptance by affiliate networks and merchants.

Here are several steps you can take to address the situation and potentially improve your chances of acceptance in the future:

Understand the Reason: Reach out to the affiliate network or merchant and politely inquire why the application was declined. This can provide valuable insights into any specific criteria or requirements you may not have met. Understanding the reason can help you address any issues or shortcomings in your application.

Improve Your Website or Content: Evaluate your website or content to ensure it meets the affiliate network or merchant's standards. Ensure your website is well-designed, user-friendly, and has high-quality content that aligns with the merchant's products or services. Enhance your website's aesthetics, navigation, and functionality if needed.

Enhance Your Traffic and Engagement: Affiliate networks and merchants often value publishers with a significant and engaged audience. Increase your website traffic, social media following, or email subscriber base. Focus on providing valuable and engaging content that attracts and retains visitors. The more active and responsive your audience, the more appealing you become to affiliate networks and merchants.

Build Your Online Presence: Establish a solid online presence by actively participating in your niche community. Engage with relevant social media groups, forums, and blogs. Collaborate with other content creators, participate in guest blogging opportunities, and network with industry professionals. Building a solid reputation and network can improve your credibility and increase your chances of acceptance.

Diversify Your Affiliate Network Applications: If one network or merchant declines your application, explore other affiliate networks or merchants that operate in your niche. Different networks may have varying criteria and requirements, so diversifying your applications can increase your chances of acceptance.

Follow Guidelines and Policies: Ensure that you thoroughly understand and adhere to the guidelines and policies of the affiliate network or merchant. Violating their terms or engaging in prohibited activities can lead to application rejections or account suspensions. Familiarize yourself with the rules and regulations to maintain a good standing with the networks and merchants you apply to.

Seek Feedback and Guidance: Seek feedback from experienced affiliate marketers or join relevant communities where you can seek guidance. Learning from others who have been successful in affiliate marketing can provide valuable insights and strategies to improve your approach.

Is Amazon Associates an excellent program to join?

Amazon Associates is considered one of the most popular and reputable affiliate marketing programs for beginners. While Amazon Associates has numerous benefits, it's also essential to consider potential limitations. For example, they have specific rules and guidelines regarding promotional methods, and their commission rates range from 1% to 10%. Additionally, some affiliates find the cookie duration, 24 hours, relatively short compared to other programs. Overall, there are hundreds of better programs to join than Amazon Associates.

What are the best affiliate marketing strategies for beginners?

For beginners in affiliate marketing, starting with practical strategies is essential to help you establish a solid foundation and achieve early success. Here are some of the best affiliate marketing strategies for beginners:

Choose a Profitable Niche: Select a niche that aligns with your interests and knowledge and has a potential audience. A niche in high demand and with room for growth can increase your chances of success.

Research and Select Reliable Affiliate Programs: Identify reputable affiliate programs that offer products or services relevant to your niche. Look for programs with a good track record, competitive commission rates, reliable tracking, and a wide range of products or services to promote.

Create Valuable Content: Focus on creating high-quality, valuable content that resonates with your target audience. Provide helpful information, tips, reviews, and recommendations for your niche. Engaging and informative content builds trust with your audience and increases their likelihood of purchasing through your affiliate links.

Build a Strong Online Presence: Establish a website or blog as a central platform for your affiliate marketing efforts. Optimize your website for search engines, create compelling landing pages, and utilize effective call-to-action. Also, leverage social media platforms to engage with your audience and drive traffic to your content.

Drive Targeted Traffic: Implement strategies to drive targeted traffic to your website. This can include search engine optimization, social media marketing, content marketing, email marketing, and paid advertising. Focus on attracting interested individuals in your niche and likely to convert them into customers.

Promote Affiliate Products Strategically: Integrate affiliate links naturally within your content and recommend products or services genuinely. Avoid excessive or intrusive promotion, as it may deter your audience. Focus on providing value and solving your audience's problems, and let affiliate promotions be a natural extension of that.

Track and Analyze Performance: Utilize tracking tools and analytics to measure the performance of your affiliate marketing efforts. Monitor your click-through rates, conversion rates, and earnings to identify what is working well and what needs improvement. This data will help you optimize your strategies and focus on the most profitable opportunities.

How should I disclose affiliate links or partnerships?

When disclosing affiliate links or partnerships, transparency and clarity are crucial. The Federal Trade Commission (FTC) in the United States requires affiliates to disclose their relationships with advertisers to ensure transparency and protect consumers. Here are a couple of examples of how you can disclose affiliate links:

Example 1 (Blog Post):

"Disclosure: This post contains affiliate links, which means that if you click on one of the product links and make a purchase, I may receive a commission. Rest assured, I only recommend products or services I genuinely believe in and have used. Your support helps me keep this blog running and delivering valuable content. Thank you!"

Example 2 (YouTube Video Description):

"Disclaimer: The links in this video description are affiliate links, which means that if you click on one of the product links and make a purchase, I may receive a small commission. This helps support the channel and allows me to continue creating videos like this. I appreciate your support!"

In both examples, it is essential to:

Mention affiliate links: Use terms like "disclosure" or "disclaimer" to state that the content contains affiliate links explicitly.

Explain the nature of affiliate links: If a user clicks on an affiliate link and makes a purchase, you may earn a commission or receive compensation.

Express genuine recommendation: Assure your audience that you only promote products or services you believe in and have personally used, emphasizing that your recommendations are based on your honest opinion.

Acknowledge the support: Thank your audience for their support, as their purchases through your affiliate links contribute to the maintenance and continuation of your content creation.

Remember, disclosure should be prominently displayed and easily noticeable to your audience. Complying with the FTC guidelines or any relevant disclosure regulations in your country or region is essential. Disclosing your affiliate relationships builds trust with your audience and ensures transparency in your affiliate marketing activities.

What are the common mistakes to avoid in affiliate marketing?

The following are mistakes to avoid in your affiliate marketing journey.

Lack of Research: Failing to conduct proper research before selecting a niche, affiliate program, or product can lead to ineffective targeting and low conversion rates. Take the time to understand your target audience, their needs, preferences, and the profitability and reputation of the affiliate programs you join.

Not Building Trust: Building trust with your audience is essential for long-term success. Avoid promoting low-quality products or services solely to earn a commission. Focus on providing value, honest recommendations, and reliable information to establish trust with your audience.

Poor Content Quality: Content is the backbone of affiliate marketing. Only publish well-written, uninformative, and relevant content. Instead, focus on creating high-quality, valuable, engaging content that resonates with your audience and encourages them to act.

Ignoring SEO: Search engine optimization drives organic traffic to your content. Ignoring SEO best practices, such as keyword research, on-page optimization, and link building, can hinder your visibility in search engine results. Incorporate SEO strategies to improve your content's visibility and attract targeted traffic.

Overlooking Disclosure: Failure to disclose your affiliate relationships can lead to legal issues and damage your credibility. Always include clear and prominent disclosures when promoting affiliate products or services. Comply with your country or region's FTC guidelines or any relevant disclosure regulations.

Spamming and Overpromotion: Bombarding your audience with excessive affiliate promotions, spamming their inboxes, or using aggressive marketing tactics can alienate your audience and harm your reputation. Instead, focus on providing value, building relationships, and recommending products or services that align with your audience's needs.

Neglecting Analytics: Tracking and analyzing your affiliate marketing performance is crucial for optimizing your strategies. Neglecting to monitor key metrics such as click-through rates, conversion rates, and earnings can hinder your ability to identify what's working and what needs improvement. Regularly review your analytics to make data-driven decisions and refine your approach.

Not Diversifying Income Sources: Relying solely on one affiliate program or traffic source can be risky. If the program or source changes its terms or experiences a decline, it could significantly impact your earnings. Diversify your income sources by joining multiple affiliate programs and exploring various traffic generation methods.

Lack of Patience and Persistence: Affiliate marketing success takes time and consistent effort. Avoid expecting overnight results or giving up too soon. Be patient, persistent, and willing to learn and adapt.

How long does it take to start earning money with affiliate marketing?

It's vital to approach affiliate marketing with a long-term mindset and realistic expectations. While some individuals may start earning money within a few months, for others, it may take six months to a year or even longer to see significant results.

The time it takes to start earning money with affiliate marketing can vary greatly depending on several factors. These factors include your level of dedication, the niche you choose, the quality of your content, the effectiveness of your marketing strategies, and the amount of traffic you generate.

Can I do affiliate marketing without a website?

It is possible to do affiliate marketing without a website, although having a website can provide many benefits and make the process more effective. Here are a few alternative methods for affiliate marketing without a website:

Social Media Platforms: Utilize social media platforms such as Instagram, Facebook, Twitter, or YouTube to promote affiliate products. Create engaging content, build a following, and share affiliate links directly on these platforms.

Email Marketing: Build an email list and use email marketing to promote affiliate products. Create valuable content and send regular newsletters or promotional emails with your affiliate links included.

YouTube Channel: Create a YouTube channel and produce video content around your niche. Embed your affiliate links in the video descriptions or mention them verbally in your videos.

Guest Blogging: Write guest posts for established blogs in your niche. Include your affiliate links within the content or author bio with the blog owner's permission.

Podcasting: Start a podcast focused on your niche and include affiliate links in the podcast episodes or show notes.

Influencer Marketing: Collaborate with influencers with a robust online presence in your niche. They can promote your affiliate links through their channels, such as social media, blogs, or YouTube.

While these methods allow you to engage in affiliate marketing without a website, remember that having a website provides more control, flexibility, and opportunities for content creation, SEO, and brand-building. It also lets you establish a central hub for affiliate marketing efforts and capture leads for future promotions. Therefore, it is recommended to have a website to enhance your affiliate marketing endeavors.

Is affiliate marketing suitable for all niches or industries?

While affiliate marketing can be applied to various niches and industries, some niches are more conducive to success than others. Here are a few factors to consider when determining if affiliate marketing is suitable for a particular niche:

Product Availability: For affiliate marketing to work effectively, there needs to be a range of products or services available for promotion within the niche. If the niche lacks relevant products or has limited affiliate programs, finding suitable offers to promote may be challenging.

Audience Demand: Assess the demand and interest of the target audience within the niche. Are people actively searching for information, products, or solutions related to the niche? Affiliate marketing can be successful if a substantial and engaged audience is seeking recommendations and solutions.

Profitability: Consider the potential for earning commissions within the niche. Some industries, such as technology, health, finance, and lifestyle, often offer higher commission rates than others. Evaluate the average order value, commission rates, and potential for recurring revenue within the niche.

Competition: Research the level of competition within the niche. While some competition can indicate a healthy market, too much competition can make it difficult to stand out and gain traction. Assess if you can differentiate yourself and offer unique value within the niche.

Align with Your Expertise and Passion: Choosing a niche that aligns with your knowledge, interests, and passion is crucial. Being familiar with the niche allows you to create valuable content, engage with the audience, and build credibility more effectively.

Long-Term Viability: Consider the long-term viability and growth potential of the niche. Is it a niche likely to thrive in the future, or is it a passing trend? Choose a niche with sustainability and potential for continued growth.

While these factors are essential to consider, with effective marketing strategies, quality content, and audience engagement, affiliate marketing can be successful in almost any niche. It may require additional creativity and effort in some niches compared to others, but with the right approach, you can find success regardless of the industry.

How can I find reputable merchants and affiliate programs and avoid scams?

Finding reputable merchants and affiliate programs requires some research and due diligence to ensure you avoid scams and work with trustworthy partners. Also, vetting potential partners will help you establish a reliable and successful affiliate marketing business while minimizing the risk of scams or fraudulent activities.

Here are some tips to help you find reputable merchants and affiliate programs:

Research Established Brands: Look for well-known and established brands in your niche or industry. Reputable companies often have affiliate programs and are more likely to offer reliable tracking, timely payments, and good customer support.

Check Affiliate Networks: Explore reputable affiliate networks such as Impact, ShareASale, CJ Affiliate, FlexOffers, and Awin. These networks vet merchants and provide a platform for affiliates to discover and join affiliate programs. They often have a wide range of reputable merchants to choose from. Remember, it doesn't cost to join an affiliate network or program. So, you should be wary if an individual or business wants to charge you to participate.

Read Reviews and Recommendations: Look for reviews and recommendations from other affiliates or industry experts. Online forums, blogs, and social media groups dedicated to affiliate marketing can be valuable sources of information and insights on reputable merchants and affiliate programs.

Research Merchant Reputation: Research the merchant's reputation before joining an affiliate program. Check for customer reviews, ratings, and negative feedback about their products or services. Ensure they have a solid track record and are known for fair business practices.

Evaluate Commission Rates and Policies: Compare commission rates offered by different affiliate programs. Be cautious if a program promises unusually high commission rates, as it could be a red flag for potential scams. Review the program's terms and policies, including cookie duration, payment thresholds, and payment methods.

Look for Affiliate Support and Resources: Reputable affiliate programs often provide affiliates with resources, promotional materials, and dedicated support. Look for programs that offer marketing materials, product data feeds, affiliate newsletters, or affiliate manager assistance.

Check Payment History and Terms: Look for information about the affiliate program's payment history and reputation for making timely payments. Review the payment terms, including payment frequency, minimum payout thresholds, and available payment methods.

Seek Transparency and Disclosures: Reputable affiliate programs are transparent about their terms, conditions, and expectations. They provide clear disclosures about affiliate relationships and comply with applicable laws and regulations, such as FTC guidelines for disclosure.

Trust Your Instincts: If something feels too good to be true or raises suspicions, trust your instincts and proceed cautiously. Avoid programs requiring upfront fees or unrealistic promises of quick and effortless wealth.

Seek Recommendations from Trusted Sources: Reach out to fellow affiliates, industry professionals, or mentors with affiliate marketing experience. They can provide valuable insights and recommendations based on their firsthand knowledge. Review social media websites and forums like Facebook and Reddit for affiliate commentary and insights.

What are the differences between affiliate marketing and multi-level marketing (MLM)?

Affiliate marketing and multi-level marketing (MLM) are two distinct business models that involve generating income through referrals and sales. Here are the key differences between affiliate marketing and MLM:

Structure and Compensation:

In affiliate marketing, affiliates earn commissions for each sale or referral they generate. They promote products or services through their online channels, and their income is directly tied to their performance.

MLM involves building a network or downline of distributors who sell products and recruit new distributors. Distributors earn commissions from their sales and the sales made by their downline. The compensation structure in MLM typically includes multiple levels or tiers, and distributors can earn additional bonuses and rewards based on their downline's performance.

Emphasis on Recruitment:

Affiliate marketers primarily promote products or services and drive sales. While they may refer others to become affiliates, the main goal is to generate sales and earn commissions from those sales.

MLM places significant emphasis on recruitment and building a network of distributors. Distributors are incentivized to recruit others and earn commissions from the sales generated by their downline. Recruitment is often a critical factor in achieving higher income levels in MLM.

Product Focus:

Affiliates typically promote specific products or services the merchant provides. They create content, reviews, or recommendations centered around those products to generate sales and earn commissions.

MLM often revolves around a broader range of products or services offered by the MLM company. Distributors are expected to sell these products and encourage their downline to do the same.

Start-up Costs and Inventory:

Affiliate marketing typically has low start-up costs since affiliates don't need to purchase inventory or invest in product development. They can join affiliate programs for free and promote products using their online platforms.

MLM frequently requires distributors to purchase a starter kit or inventory upfront, which can involve a significant investment. Distributors may need to maintain a list of products to sell or distribute to their customers.

Business Independence:

Affiliates operate independently and have control over their promotional strategies, content creation, and online presence. They are not tied to a specific company and can promote products from multiple merchants or affiliate networks.

MLM distributors are typically associated with a specific MLM company and must adhere to its rules, policies, and marketing guidelines. They are more closely tied to the MLM company's brand and product offerings.

Affiliate marketing is widely regarded as a legitimate and sustainable business model; MLM has been associated with controversies and legal issues due to concerns about pyramid schemes and deceptive practices. Aspiring entrepreneurs should carefully research and understand the differences between these models to make informed decisions about the type of business they want to pursue.

What are the differences between affiliate marketing and dropshipping?

Affiliate marketing and drop shipping are popular business models with distinct characteristics, pros, and cons. Affiliate marketing offers a low barrier to entry, requires minimal investment, and allows for passive income generation. On the other hand, drop shipping provides more control over product selection, pricing, and customer experience but involves more operational responsibilities. Entrepreneurs should consider their preferences, resources, and goals when deciding which model aligns best with their business aspirations.

The key differences between affiliate marketing and dropshipping are as follows:

Product Ownership and Inventory:
In affiliate marketing, affiliates promote products or services owned and managed by the merchant. Affiliates don't handle the products themselves or have any responsibility for inventory management. When a sale is made through their referral, they earn a commission from the merchant.

With dropshipping, the business owner acts as a middleman between the customer and the supplier. The business owner lists products on their online store, but they don't physically own the products or keep inventory. When a customer makes a purchase, the order is forwarded to the supplier, who ships the product directly to the customer.

Order Fulfillment and Shipping:
Affiliates are not involved in order fulfillment or shipping. Once a customer clicks on their affiliate link and makes a purchase, the merchant handles all aspects of order processing, including packaging, shipping, and customer service.

Dropshipping businesses are responsible for coordinating the order fulfillment process. When a customer orders, the business owner forwards the order details to the supplier, who then ships the product directly to the customer. The business owner is responsible for customer service and handling any issues that may arise during the shipping process.

Control Over Products and Pricing:
Affiliates have no control over the products or their pricing. The merchant determines the product offering, pricing, and discounts or promotions. Affiliates promote the products using the provided affiliate links but do not influence the product details or pricing.

Dropshipping business owners have more control over product selection and pricing. They can curate their product catalog, set prices, and adjust product offerings based on market demand. This gives them the flexibility to experiment with different products and pricing strategies.

Customer Relationship:

In affiliate marketing, affiliates drive traffic and refer customers to the merchant's website. Once the customer purchases, the merchant is responsible for the ongoing customer relationship, including order support, customer service, and any potential follow-up marketing.

Dropshipping business owners have more direct interaction with customers since they handle customer inquiries, order status updates, and any post-sale support. This allows for a more personalized customer experience and the opportunity to build a direct relationship with customers.

Profit Margin:

Affiliates earn a commission on each sale made through their affiliate link, typically a percentage of the sale price. The commission rates can vary, but they are usually lower than the profit margin in dropshipping.

Dropshipping business owners have the potential for higher profit margins since they can set their prices and negotiate favorable terms with suppliers. The difference between the supplier's cost and the price charged to the customer contributes to the business owner's profit.

That concludes the information in this book. Please leave a review on Amazon at your earliest convenience. We would appreciate your support.

Good luck with your affiliate marketing activities, and I hope you reach your first $10,000 in commissions sooner than later.

Made in the USA
Coppell, TX
14 July 2025

51868950R00069